Journey to Heaven

Praise for
Journey to Heaven

For over sixty years, *Thanatopsis* by William Cullen Bryant has been one of my favorite poems. Now *Journey to Heaven* shows you the way to "approach thy grave like one who wraps the drapery of his couch about him and lies down to pleasant dreams.
—C. Norman Shealy, MD, PhD
founding President, American Holistic Medical Association
author of *Energy Medicine: The Future of Health*

Journey to Heaven is a unique and engaging book that gives specific answers to questions you have always had about the afterlife. If you have ever speculated about All That Is and want to understand what is on the other side, this book will give you valuable insights. Your quest for understanding will be enhanced by the higher perspective contained in these pages.
—Stanley Krippner, PhD
past President, Association for Humanistic Psychology
coauthor of *Personal Mythology*

This breakthrough work redefines what people have previously believed about heaven and the process of dying. Anne's connection to the energy she calls All That Is helps clear the haze of human confusion, sharing information that brings insights and clarity. *Journey to Heaven* makes one thing clear: our transition is determined by our beliefs and our thoughts. What we believe to be real becomes our reality.
—Pia Orleane, PhD and Cullen Smith
authors of *Conversations with Laarkmaa*
and *Remembering Who We Are*

Anne Salisbury and Greg Meyerhoff invite you to join them in a truly remarkable adventure. As Physsie, Anne's mother, was standing at the doorway of death, they planned how the three of them would write this book about crossing over and the afterlife. Physsie concentrated on what was happening along her path before and after her death. Greg asked questions of Physsie and All That Is, who both communicated through Anne. Whatever your present view of life after death or channeling, exploring this amazing book will leave you better informed. It includes excellent exercises if you care to go deeper.

—Robert Nunley, PhD
Dean of Faculty, Holos University Graduate Seminary
Professor Emeritus of Geography, University of Kansas

This wonderful book is long overdue for those of us who have looked for this knowledge to be revealed. Through Physsie's experience of death, we have learned that you make choices throughout your transitioning process. You can also live better on both sides through staying more connected to your higher self. This book can truly help you live more fully and feel more comfortable in your transition. I couldn't put it down and will read it again.

—Joan Putthoff, MA, MEd
former Benedictine nun
former Professor, University of Missouri – Kansas City

Journey to Heaven is very positive and uplifting. And it's so informative yet personal with Physsie's input. I especially like having the exercises available at the back of the book. It's terrific!

—Debbie Meloy
forty-year meditator, Transcendental Meditation
and TM-Sidhi Program

It is rare to find inspired writing presented in down-to-earth language with insights sprinkled liberally throughout—insights that actually make you think differently! The book you now hold is such a creation.

Journey to Heaven promises to change the way you understand death. If you've had a loved one die and wondered how it was for them or if you've been thinking about your own death and how it might be for you, you will find great comfort and light in these pages. I learned some important things from this book—things that actually made me deeply *happy*!

—from the Foreword by Penney Peirce
author of *Frequency* and *Leap of Perception*

Bravo! Under the gentle guidance of All That Is, Anne, Greg, and Physsie have pioneered a writing collaboration to produce an inspiring, entertaining, and deeply insightful guidebook on making the transition we call dying less of a mystery.

Their commitment to loving one another and collaborating on a book after Physsie's death has brought about this heartwarming and life-enriching illumination of a human experience that is so often shrouded in darkness and dread. Contrary to the pervasive fear that dying brings about loss of relationship and further isolation, the authors illustrate that dying is a celebration of life. Until we fully realize that there is, in truth, no death, we must not shy away from exploring the dying process.

As we consistently apply what we learn to full participation in both our own and others' dying and death, we discover that what we call death is but our wakeup call to life. So don't wait until you are on your deathbed. If you seek to live more fully, read this book now!

—Michael J. Tamura
author of *You Are The Answer*

Beyond informative and fascinating, *Journey to Heaven* is an experience. You feel the lifting of vibrational energies as you read it. It is filled with useful analogies that make challenging concepts easy to understand. I am especially appreciative of the supportive exercises that keep the experience of this book alive. This is a beautiful gift of love from Anne, Greg, Physsie, and All That Is.

—Melanie Smithson, MA, LPC, BC-DMT, CHt
Certified Life Between Lives Hypnotherapist
author of *Stress Free in 30 Seconds*

Also Available
by Anne Salisbury and Greg Meyerhoff

Books
Eureka! Understanding and Using the Power of Your Intuition
The Path of Intuition: Your Guidebook for Life's Journey

CDs and DVDs
How to Be More Aware in Relationships (lecture CD)
Intuition Explained through Stories (lecture CD)
Your Ideal Body (self-hypnosis CD)
Weight Management: Lecture & Demonstration (DVD)

Distance Learning Courses
Intuitive Skills I: Tools for Life
Intuitive Skills II: Tools for Inner Sight
Intuitive Skills for Relationships
Intuitive Skills for Creating What You Want

Visit GoIntuition.com for
• Books and downloads.
• Talks and trainings on intuition.
• Business consulting for decision making.
• Intuitive coaching for relationships, work, health.
• Energy clearing/feng shui for home, business.
• Pet psychic readings.
• Communicating with loved ones on the other side.

Visit TranspersonalHypnotherapyInstitute.com for
• CDs, DVDs, distance learning courses.
• Certification trainings in hypnotherapy, intuition.
• Transpersonal Hypnotherapy, Past Life Regression.

Order this book from your bookseller or
GoIntuition.com

Conversations with All That Is

Journey to Heaven

An Insider's Guide to the Afterlife

Anne Salisbury, PhD

Greg Meyerhoff

Foreword by Penney Peirce

Journey to Heaven
An Insider's Guide to the Afterlife
By Anne Salisbury, PhD and Greg Meyerhoff
Visit *GoIntuition.com*

Publisher's Cataloging-in-Publication
(Provided by Quality Books, Inc.)
Salisbury, Anne, author, medium.
    Journey to heaven : an insider's guide to the afterlife : conversations with All That Is / Anne Salisbury, Greg Meyerhoff ; foreword by Penney Peirce.
    pages cm
    LCCN 2016901899
    ISBN 978-0-9758509-7-8 (paperback)
    ISBN 978-0-9758509-8-5 (ebook)
    1. Future life. 2. Spiritualism. 3. Spirit writings. 4. All That Is (Spirit)
I. Meyerhoff, Greg, author. II. All That Is (Spirit) III. Title.
    BF1261.2.S265 2016   133.901'3
                     QBI16-600058

Book design by Nick Zelinger
Editing by Melanie Mulhall
Published in USA by Lively Spirit, Inc.

Books may be purchased in quantity by contacting the publisher:
Lively Spirit, Inc.,
P. O. Box 18409, Golden, Colorado 80402, USA
LivelySpirit.com
info@LivelySpirit.com

This book is dedicated to you, our readers, who forge ahead desiring to make this life and the afterlife a better experience. We appreciate you for doing this. May you walk the path to heaven with joy.

Contents

Foreword by Penney Peirce 15

Introduction 21

PART ONE: Beginning the Journey 25

Chapter 1: Physsie's Story 27

Chapter 2: Opt-Out Points 29

Chapter 3: Looking for Home 37

Chapter 4: People in the Room 41

Chapter 5: Choosing When to Cross Over 45

Chapter 6: Completing and the Completion Team 51

Chapter 7: Events in the Final Days 57

Chapter 8: The Transition Process 61

PART TWO: Crossing Over and Getting Situated 67

Chapter 9: Making the Crossing 69

Chapter 10: Recuperation 75

Chapter 11: Your Higher Self and Recuperation 83

Chapter 12: The Fracturing of Energy 87

Chapter 13: Energy Retrieval 93

Chapter 14: Touring the Other Side 99

Chapter 15: Seeing Family and Friends 107

Chapter 16: Life Review 113

PART THREE: Releasing Negativity 121

Chapter 17: Negative Beliefs and Thought Forms 123

Chapter 18: Gremlin Energy 129

Chapter 19: Grappling with Gremlins 139
Chapter 20: Loneliness and Lack Attract Gremlins 145

PART FOUR: Guidance and Support 153
Chapter 21: Your Higher Self 155
Chapter 22: Spirit Guides 163
Chapter 23: Angels, Archangels, and Guardian Angels . . 171
Chapter 24: Heaven 181

Appendix A: Energy Exercises 189
Appendix B: Key Words and Phrases 197
Appreciation 207
About the Authors 209
Learn More 211
Discover *Eureka!* 212
Discover *The Path of Intuition* 213
Coming Soon 214

Foreword

by Penney Peirce

Channeled writings became popular back in the 1980s around the time I was opening up spiritually to my work as a professional intuitive. I've known many good trance mediums, whose work was profound, and have also been flooded with missives from well-meaning "channelers" and those who wanted validation for their special personal connection with St. Germain, Star Beings from Orion, or Jesus. So much of the content in this type of writing tended to be broad and general and dictated in the formal sentence structure of some old English lord, Egyptian high priest, or Native American shaman.

It is rare to find inspired writing presented in down-to-earth language with insights sprinkled liberally throughout—insights that actually make you think differently! The book you now hold is such a creation. It promises to change the way you understand death. You'll come away realizing that life is really all there is. There is physical life and nonphysical life and we, as souls, simply rock in and out whenever we wish.

I've been exploring the process of dying and the after-death experience for as long as I can remember. It never occurred to me, even as a child, that death was "the end" or that upon leaving the body, it all just goes black and consciousness ceases to be. The concepts of life after death and reincarnation were as logical and normal as eating and drinking. It seemed to me that it was important, though, to understand how to die consciously, without struggle or contraction, and that if we could do that, we'd dissolve much of our fear and bring more of our memory with us into the nonphysical world so we'd be able to bring it back

15

in our next lifetime. That way we wouldn't need to dramatize our lessons all over again. Why reinvent the wheel?

As I became a professional intuitive, I constantly kept an inner eye open for hints about how to die consciously, how to stay present through the process, and how to remove suffering from the equation. I wanted to know what happens in the after-death stages of accommodating oneself once again to the fast, frictionless reality that occurs when the body and the residual negative emotions held by the body don't weigh us down any longer.

I was incredibly lucky in the early years of my spiritual awakening to become friends with an amazing full trance medium, Dollee Campbell, who died a few years ago. She told me in great detail—as though reading out of an encyclopedia—about many of my recent past lives, which I was able to find record of after the internet came into being. One of those lives was as a woman writer in the mid-1800s, Alice Cary, who died of tuberculosis at age fifty. As I researched her, I found many of her poems and stories, as well as uncanny parallels to my own writings and life. In one poem, she writes, "Laugh, you who never had / Your dead come back; / but do not take from me / The harmless comfort of my foolish dream: / That these our mortal eyes, / Which outwardly reflect the earth and skies, / Do introvert upon eternity." And in another, "My friend, wilt thou lend me thy counsel? / And then, if thou wilt, we will strive / O'er the river of death to build bridges, / That souls may o'erpass it and live." And one more, "Our deaths are but mystic stops / In the great melody of love." I can't help but wonder if my interest in conscious dying was strengthened by Cary's own conscious death.

Finding the common threads that weave through my lives has been a big help in reaffirming my intuitions that we absolutely do have continuing consciousness and that our soul operates seamlessly day and night and during our physical and nonphysical experiences. I have come to see death as a simple blinking out of a way of experiencing life at a particular frequency and blinking in to another higher frequency perception where life doesn't fracture into time, space, and objects but functions as a much smoother continuum. I've experienced firsthand, in visions, dreams, and meditations, some of the ways the process of dying works. I can say that the Flow knows what it's doing and if we can learn to become one with it, and trust it, we will be guided through the transition experience quite smoothly.

All this to say that it didn't surprise me much when Anne and Greg's manuscript came across my desk. My mother, age ninety-three, had just died a few short weeks before! I was in the midst of processing the way she had feared and stubbornly resisted the idea of dying, refusing to talk about it at all, then how she gradually pulled out in stages by weakening herself. It was as though she had to trick her mind and make herself miserable enough that she would finally let go. Helping her through the last weeks was an ordeal, and there was much suffering. At last she had a stroke (at the "stroke" of midnight) and went to the hospital, where inattention and bumbling treatment, including putting her in restraints in her last hours, probably convinced her to "get out of Dodge" and "give up the ghost."

What is so great about *Journey to Heaven* is that it documents various aspects and stages of what many of us may experience before, during, and after the experience we call death. To me, it's extraordinarily helpful to have the perspective of people who have died and experienced the full process without memory loss, and who can speak clearly about it from the nonphysical state. So much of what comes forth from All That Is through Anne

Salisbury is compassionate, healing, interesting—and specific. This speaks to Anne's emotional and mental maturity and to Anne's and Greg's clear phrasing of questions that can elicit not just platitudes but detailed information. The information in this book is supremely reassuring and resonates with everything I've ever received intuitively myself. As I was reading through the material, my intuition continued to validate the content Anne was receiving. I learned some important things from this book—things that actually made me deeply *happy*!

We operate on two levels during our lifetimes: basically, our outer personality/physical self often succumbs to fear and peer pressure to participate in suffering and acts protectively to ensure survival. Our inner, eternal soul-self is connected to the evolving Flow and all other beings and is unfailingly clear about what it wants to materialize here on Earth, and how easy it is to do just that. It knows no fear. Our spiritual growth is a process of regaining memory of who we really are, of merging our soul and personality, and of seeing the physical world as the spiritual world—what Anne and Greg call All That Is—and completely dissolving fear back into the unified field of compassion and joy.

So often, the outer self blocks the inner self and distorts our understanding. That is especially true of the process of dying. Our personalities are hesitant to look and feel into what actually occurs, and that leads to seeing death as loss rather than gain. *Journey to Heaven* helps us see that the physical and nonphysical worlds aren't separate, that dying isn't frightening, that there is no loss, and that the Flow is our friend. This book shows us that the reality of our personality can soften so we can read between the lines, or see through the thinning veil, to find the sanity and purposefulness in how souls set up their transition between frequencies and states of being.

I recall that on the last night of my mother's life, I went back to the hospital alone after dinner and sat in the dimmed room with her. She was propped up so she could breathe more easily and I told her I loved her and other important things, cried, and for a while, just sat in silence with her, holding her hand. At one point she looked me straight in the eyes, very seriously, and started talking in the gibberish that was the result of the stroke. She probably thought it was coming out intelligibly and kept on and on. I knew she was saying all the "big" things she'd never said to me, so I just kept acknowledging her. At some level I knew it was all getting through. Even though this was happening, and I knew it was the big stuff one usually says in the last moments, I didn't have a conscious inkling that she would die in a few hours. She was so strong and she constantly rallied from setbacks.

Finally, she was calm. I told her we'd be back first thing in the morning and to please get some good rest. I said that I knew it had been a torturous day for her but it would all be okay. I had a sense to *not* stay in the room with her overnight. As I walked to the door, I turned and blew her a kiss. She puckered her lips, raised two fingers, and wiggled them at me: Good-bye. I went through the door with the sudden thought that this was the last time I'd see her. Immediately my left brain chimed in. *Oh, no! She's strong. We'll take this up in the morning and see what can be done to clear the blood clot.* She slipped away around four in the morning.

Thinking back on this last scene now, I am clear how we both pretended not to know she was going to leave that night. We both intuitively knew—without knowing that we knew—that she wanted to be unencumbered by her own and other people's emotions so she could leave her body peacefully when the night was at its quietest point. And we both said good-bye to each other in that casual, sweet way—without consciously acknowledging how final it really was—as though we'd surely see each other again, very soon. Our souls' compassion in that small exchange is still fairly excruciating to me when I feel it.

It is this sort of realization—how souls cooperate with each other, and support each other, to minimize fear and make the experience of passing as compassionate and easy as possible—that *Journey to Heaven* helps us understand. If you've had a loved one die and wondered how it was for them or if you've been thinking about your own death and how it might be for you, you will find great comfort and light here in these pages.

—Penney Peirce
Author of *Frequency* and *Leap of Perception*

Introduction

What would it be like if you knew heaven before you arrived there? What if you felt you had options in transitioning? What if you really knew what it was like to cross over to the other side? You would probably feel a tremendous sense of calm and ease in your life, and you would likely have more confidence. It would make your life on Earth and your afterlife more enjoyable, and you would be more enlightened as you walked your own path to heaven.

Heaven is what you make of it. Depending on your level of awareness, you can determine your options before and after you arrive on the other side. If you want to be supported in a loving transition, then you create loving beings on both sides who help you anyway they can. If you are expecting pearly gates or a judgment day in the afterlife, then you can create that too. If you don't really know what you want, then your beliefs and unconscious thoughts will create your world for you, and you can be surprised when you arrive in heaven.

Just like Earth, heaven is a real place. It is an oasis where you refresh yourself, recuperate from your journeys, and prepare for your next adventure. You might decide to continue learning on Earth through reincarnation or you might choose to explore another reality. It all depends on what kind of experience you want to have next. As you gain more awareness, you have more options.

What you do while you are alive dramatically affects your experience on the other side. You take your wisdom with you. The more healing you do on Earth, the less you need to do over there. Issues only go away after you resolve them. If you begin your journey to heaven now, you can make your life, your transition, and your arrival on the other side much more enjoyable.

In the following pages, we explore the journey to heaven from two main viewpoints. As professional intuitives, we share firsthand accounts from Anne's mother and others who have recently passed, which we received clairvoyantly. We also give you the higher perspective of All That Is as intuitively channeled through Anne.

This information may stretch you, and that's a good thing. Let's use Disneyland as an example. You go there to have some laughs, rest, and rejuvenate. You know it is a contrived reality and yet you still appreciate it for what it offers you. You can stay for a day or a week, depending on what you need to feel better. You know there are behind-the-scenes activities not obvious to the average ticket buyer, but initially, you do not care about the mechanics of the place as long as you have a good time. If you become curious, you might want to know how the Disney characters seemingly appear out of nowhere. And you might be surprised to learn that they often use underground passage-ways and secret doors. Just in case there is an emergency, it would be good to know about the exit doors. And the more you see, the more you might want to know. It is the same with heaven. A little education can take you a long way.

Through these pages, you will be shown where the potholes are so you can avoid them. Like travel guides, we will let you know what you can expect ahead. Life and the afterlife can be so enjoyable when you are well prepared for your journey. Heaven is still heaven, the place you go when you die, but it may just be a little different than you thought it would be.

Channeling All That Is

Journey to Heaven is based on channeled material. Channeling can be described as accessing information through intuition. Anne accesses universal wisdom that is beyond our everyday understanding through channeling aspects of All That Is. She responds to Greg's questions of her when she is in trance. The answers given by All That Is often inspire us to contemplate the core of our being and the reality we create around us. They have made themselves available to us to expand our awareness and assist us, as a people, in our evolution in consciousness.

The whole of All That Is emanates from Source and is in all things. Anne communicates telepathically with a portion of the whole, which could be said to be a group consciousness of nonphysical energy that comes from a place and time distant from our general experience. They offer loving wisdom from a higher vibration of awareness.

Authors' Note

All That Is refer to themselves in the plural. For example, they will say, "We suggest . . . ." They also refer to humans in the plural when they say, "You." Know they are speaking to you.

Because we asked the questions and gave you the answers from All That Is, we know there are always more questions to ask. When we ask a question with one intention, we may receive an answer and then ask the same question again with a different intention and receive a different answer, representing a different perspective. We usually ask follow-up questions to delve deeper into a subject. The learning is ongoing. In each section, you will find questions asked in a variety of ways.

You may assume that it is All That Is answering the questions unless we note otherwise. For the sake of readability, we have not put either our questions or the answers given by All That Is in quotes. However, when an answer is given by someone else on the other side, we have placed the material in quotes to clearly differentiate it from the answers given by All That Is.

Know that there is tremendous support for you on the other side. We have felt this support, and our views on what is possible have expanded tremendously through this investigative experience. We recommend that you, too, call on your higher self to help you intuit and integrate this material as you go.

May this book assist you in having a better life on this side and the other.

—Anne Salisbury and Greg Meyerhoff

PART ONE

Beginning the Journey

Your universe is yours to create on this side and the other.

According to All That Is, you have a unique journey in life, and this uniqueness also applies to your transition to the other side. The activities you experience in your transition may be similar to someone else's, yet you may interpret them differently because you come from your own personal perspective. In contrast, you may each participate in different activities on the other side but interpret them similarly because you come from similar cultures or religions. Your belief system plays a significant role in your experience on the other side.

In the following pages, some of the experiences are described as separate events in a logical timeline. This is to make them easier to understand. Actually, some of these separate events occur simultaneously, and there is a mingling and fluidity of experiences.

Chapter 1

Physsie's Story

What transpired was a miracle.

"**A**re you in there?" Physsie shouted with her face planted inches above mine, awakening me with a start. Shortly after she had passed, and I was still catching up on sleep after the ordeal. This was not a dream. She was contacting me.

As a professional psychic, I was accustomed to being awakened by clients and friends from the other side. And I had made an agreement with Physsie, my ninety-year-old mother, to keep in contact after she passed. She was keeping up with her end of the bargain.

We had already experienced some strange events with her passing such as the doorbell, lights, and alarm clocks going on and off. Then a few days after Physsie died in late December, her friend Joan called me. I had been searching for Joan since March, but no one knew where she was. Her phone was disconnected and mail to her was returned. I had even searched the internet to see if she had died and found her brother's obituary, which had been posted months earlier. The funeral home would not provide any information, so in November, I posted on its site that I was looking for Joan because my mother, her dear friend who was getting close to dying, wanted to connect.

What transpired was a miracle. Someone saw the note on that site, anonymously called the nursing home where Joan was living temporarily, and had her call me. When I answered the phone, the fire alarm in my home-office went off. Shortly after that, the lights went on and off in the room that had been Physsie's bedroom the last three years of her life. Physsie was telling us she was pleased that we had finally connected with Joan and said she played a part in that reunion from the other side.

Before her death, Physsie said she really didn't want to die because she had so much to do. She enjoyed editing our books and materials. So we made an agreement and shook on it. We would write a book with her about her experiences on the other side after she became situated over there.

About six months after her transition, I had a clear vision-like dream in which Physsie showed up at the front door in her underwear. I was shocked. "Physsie, how did you get here?" I asked.

"I drove," she replied.

"Really?" I said, incredulous. "That's impressive. You haven't driven in years, and here you drove in your underpants."

"I know. I'm impressed myself," she admitted. "But here I am, and I'm ready to get going on our book. It's time to get at it."

The next day we actively started communicating with her directly to get her perspective on the other side. We wanted to know what it is like to transition, from an insider's perspective, and she could provide that.

Thanks to Physsie's communication, along with guidance from All That Is, death and the other side are no longer a mystery to us. What we have learned through our investigation has put the puzzle pieces together for us in ways that have been enlightening and even, at times, surprising.

Chapter 2

Opt-Out Points

Your opt-out points give you flexibility.
This is a kindness you give yourself in
your experiments you call life.

As spirit, there are certain goals you want to accomplish when you incarnate into physical form. These goals can be ambitious or easy depending on your decisions. For instance, if you had a tough lifetime the last go-around, you might choose a calm life to recuperate. If, however, you want to advance quickly to a higher level of consciousness, you might design a challenging life for yourself to get it all done.

As each goal on Earth is completed, you come to a choice point where you have options. These are called your "opt-out points." You can either finish things and pass over or you can continue with your life and accomplish your next goal. Events, big and small, allow you to look at your life and make choices about your future.

The opt-out point you use as your exit point is a negotiated decision between your full self, your higher self, and your personality. Your full self's opinion ultimately carries the greatest weight.

Question: All That Is, could you talk about opt-out points?

There are many times when you can choose to remove yourself from this reality that you call life. The more you grow and challenge yourself, the more opportunities you give yourself to exit in case things become too rough or you accomplish your predetermined tasks early. This means you drop your body, move on, regroup on the other side, and reenter through another body to have a life experience again. This allows you fluidity of movement.

Those who have not incarnated much consider fewer options in their planning. They are not as aware of the potential opt-out points available to them. They feel they must complete a task, and once that task is complete, they leave their body. They design simpler life plans with fewer tasks and fewer options.

But when you have experienced many incarnations, you may design five, six, or possibly seven opportunities to drop your body and move on in one lifetime. You might say to yourself, "Oh, let me see. I could finish this task here and that task there. I may desire to move on, but I may be enjoying myself so much that I don't want to leave, so I want to give myself options." You could also have a simpler lifetime and say, "Oh, I give myself one, two, or three potential times when I might die and regroup."

This allows you, as spirit, flexibility. Before you incarnate into a body, when you review the possibilities for that lifetime, you know there is a great likelihood that certain circumstances will unfold. But you do not know how you, as a physical being, will react to those circumstances. That is part of the adventure. You want to discover how you, as a spirit with a body, will respond. You want to succeed in your self-assigned tasks. This is your discovery project.

It is like being a scientist in a laboratory. You are experimenting. If your experiment goes awry, you want the opportunity to repeat that experiment with slight alterations. You may be able to redo that experiment in your current lifetime with your current body by introducing a different person or different circumstances to change things around a bit.

But in your review of the future possibilities, if you determine it is unlikely that life circumstances will allow you to fulfill your desires or tasks, you have choices. You either decide to move on to the next life to recreate your experiment there or you say to yourself, "You know, I have a list of other things I would also like to experience, so I choose to move on to my next experiment and will return to this one in my next lifetime."

When you are quite creative, you may say, "Oh, look. I have a grand list, so I will keep moving on to my next task," which might be task three, four, or five. In this way, you are flexible in what you desire to experience. The longer you are at it, the more likely you will recognize when your body can rally and you can be creative when opt-out points present themselves to you. It is all a matter of choice.

Question: How do you design a task for yourself when you incarnate?

You decide to complete a task in a particular area to fulfill a desire you have. A task, for example, might be to love yourself more in relationship. You tell yourself, "I have been unable to receive love from a romantic partner for some time. Long ago, I made decisions that blocked my ability to receive. The last few lifetimes I have had, I have felt unfulfilled. I felt that my partner did not love me, even though I did everything I could to be loved. So in this lifetime, I would like to receive a glimmer of hope that I am loved. I would like to have at least a moment during which I am the recipient of romantic appreciation. I desire to replace the belief that I am unworthy of romantic love with the feeling that I am worthy."

So you incarnate desiring to have an experience in which you feel loved by a romantic partner. That is the first task you set in front of yourself. Then you may set up a second task around business relationships. You have felt betrayed by business partners over and over again. You felt they, too, did not see your worth, and you desire to feel successful in a business partnership.

Task number three might be to receive love from a pet and return it in equal quantities. In the past, you may have looked after animals but felt distant from them or used them without seeing them as your equals and your companions. In your heart, you now desire that experience of companionship.

From the other side you say to yourself, "These are my three desires for this coming lifetime. Truly, I may have bitten off more than I can chew, so if I have not felt love from a romantic partner by the time I am fifty years old, I will give myself the option to opt out. I do not know if I can handle hanging on much longer than that hoping to accomplish my task."

Then you say, "But if there is a glimmer of hope when I am fifty, I will give myself another few years to see how I am doing. If I have accomplished my task by the time I am fifty-five, I can choose to leave, for I will feel fulfilled. I can also choose to continue to task number two and further enjoy myself."

In other words, your opt-out points can be for having accomplished your tasks or not having accomplished them. You can retreat to the other side to bask in your accomplishments and design new tasks for yourself or you can opt out after being unable to accomplish all that you desired. Then it is time to regroup and recuperate on the other side and start designing your next life.

Your opt-out points give you flexibility. This is a kindness you give yourself in your experiments you call life. They are not meant to hurt those around you because you choose to go. You can regroup and try again while you are in physical form or you can regroup on the other side with a larger perspective on your possibilities.

Another possibility for completing your tasks is through your dreams. You can review your possibilities, experiment with options, and renew yourself in your dream state. By asking your higher self to help you during sleep, you can create and change your approach to life in a gentle way.

Question: *After being married only four years, Physsie's first husband, Beach, died in an auto accident at age thirty-two. Did he opt out?*

Yes. You could say that Beach desired to accomplish certain things in this lifetime. He wanted to feel good about himself, so he became a successful businessperson and was well appreciated by those at his work. He wanted to find a wife he could love thoroughly and who could love and appreciate him, which he did in marrying Physsie. He also desired to feel loved and appreciated by his parents, and he accomplished this.

He felt he was on task and had accomplished much, so he desired to pass over and review how far he had come. He did not mean to hurt the ones he loved. By exiting in a car crash, he made his transition quite swiftly, and when he returned to the other side, he saw how many suffered from his death. He desired to return to Physsie, but he knew he must be strong and allow those in his reality to heal themselves however they desired to do that. He knew they, too, had the desire to grow and be strong, so he stepped back.

This was part of his big lesson, which was to be strong and to allow others to be strong without being there to rescue them. It was a challenge for him, but it was the desired design. Accomplishing tasks is often hard on the emotional body. That difficulty is reflected in the physical body too. But on the level of spirit, it is a gift you give yourself to grow—to experience what it is like to be a fulfilled being, one who has accomplished the tasks you placed in front of yourself.

Question: What were Physsie's tasks?

Physsie desired to see herself as whole and love herself more. But she forgot she could do that herself and, instead, thought another had to complete her. She thought Beach had to be the reflection of love that made her whole and forgot she was whole no matter what the circumstances were around her.

In her tasks to see herself as whole and love herself more, she kept feeling grief over the loss of her husband. This grief clouded her reality. It made her unable to see herself as whole or loved in the physical realm. She rejected love from another romantic partner because she desired her Beach to return. But he could not because his agreement was to allow her to grow alone. He knew that she would lean on him if he was in her reality.

When her opt-out points appeared, she chose to remain in this reality to give herself the opportunity to grow. This was admirable, for she had been through so much and her emotional body was wounded. However, in her woundedness and grief, she unintentionally allowed energies that were impure to enter her system to help her feel loved and whole. Those energies told her they could make her feel better, but truly, they could not.

They told her that if she ate sugar, she would feel sweetness again. This artificial reality did not last and did not satisfy her desire to feel self-love. It masked the real situation, and sugar addiction occurred. The addiction to sugar is quite common in your world. It is the artificial feeling of love. It stimulates that part of you that feels good, but only in the physical form. In the realm of spirit, it represents an incomplete task. You could say that Physsie had ingested a lie, and this made it difficult for her to find herself because her reality was clouded by lies.

In the end, her higher self recognized she would be unable to fulfill her task of loving herself more if she remained in physical form. She had to release the energies that were committed to help her in what was truly an unhealthy way. She had to break those unconscious agreements so she could accomplish her tasks herself. It was time to regroup on the other side.

Question: Was Physsie aware of her opt-out points?

She says she was aware of four or five of them. She could have committed suicide after Beach died, but that would have caused trauma to those around her, especially her parents. She could have left at the announcement of her second husband's affairs, but she chose to remain for her children. She could have left after her divorce when she came down with leukemia, but she chose to stay because she was on a journey to discover herself. This took great strength of spirit.

In 2007, she could have crossed over when she collapsed with an infection, but when you two came to her rescue, you showed her you held so much love in your hearts for her that she wanted to create love for herself. Your selfless acts of love showed her she was worthy of more love. You showed her possibilities. This occurred again in 2009 when another infection landed her in the hospital and you helped her in her sickened state. She realized she could love herself more and became determined to do so.

Later, when she was losing her mind through dementia and her body was falling apart, she wanted to opt out. That is why she desired to bring in hospice. She wanted help to die and also felt a team effort could contribute to her sense of self-love. This assistance fulfilled her and gave her the strength to move on to the other side. She felt supported. There are so many ways an individual can choose to opt out. These are simply a few examples from Physsie's life.

Question: Was Physsie able to love herself more in the final years by sticking around?

No, not exactly. In those last years, her dementia clouded her mind and unseen energies tried to control her. She was able to appreciate herself more during her last week. She was able to release the negative energy beings that had attached themselves to her because she had not been present in her body. In her transition, the love she felt for herself and others was tremendous, and she felt more complete and whole. She also felt there was more to be done. We recognize this and honor that she accomplished much in her world through her choices to continue when she might have opted out.

Chapter 3

Looking for Home

Love has no location because it is everywhere
at all times. Home is simply a feeling
of goodness, appreciation, completion,
and wholeness.

"Where is my home?" Physsie kept asking. That last month, she wandered around the house looking puzzled asking, "Where am I? These are my things, but this is not my home. How did my furniture get here?"

"We brought it here in a truck," we replied.

"Thank you for all your efforts," she said, "but this is not my home."

Physsie was sleeping most of the time now. This allowed her to visit the other side more and build her home there. When she opened her eyes and saw her things in our home, she became confused because a part of her had already moved everything to the other side. She would make her bed and sit on the edge of it, waiting to go.

One night, while she barely had the strength left to stand, she got up, carefully made her bed, and said, "I'm not sure whose place this is, but I have to leave. Where are my suitcases? Where are my shoes and clothes? I have to pack. Please thank whoever runs this fine establishment for having us, but I have to go home."

Question: In the last few weeks before Physsie died, she kept getting out of bed and walking around the house saying she wanted to go home. Hospice says this is common at the end of life. Could you please explain?

Towards the end there was an urge to find herself, to find her truth. She needed to locate herself within her heart as a being of light. To her, home was the center of her universe, and her universe was herself. She desired to go inward and experience that she was God, creator in her realm.

Agitation arose within her when she looked outside for answers. The answers were not there, and the part of her that was wise knew that. She could not find home in her physical reality. Yet, when she closed her eyes, went inside, and knew that she was her own God, she was satisfied and quieted down.

This is the search for home. Home is inside of you. It is that small, still place near your heart, behind it, where you reside as spirit when you incarnate in form. It is where you may see yourself as the spark of light that is who you truly are. You reside in stillness as that being of light in the great void you call love.

Love has no location because it is everywhere at all times. Home is simply a feeling of goodness, appreciation, completion, and wholeness. It is where you feel loved and where there is no lack. It is a grand experience, a vibration in which you allow yourself to relax and know you are God, a creator, a spark of light held in fabric of love.

Question: What was Physsie's experience of looking for home?

Physsie says that everything was falling apart. Her reality was crumbling and nothing made sense. You could see it as a wall that is falling apart in front of you. You are watching the stones and mortar fall to the ground. Nothing is organized and nothing makes sense.

When she opened her eyes, she saw some things that made sense, such as her bureau and chair, but they were out of place in her mind. She thought they belonged in another home from another time. To her, everything had been thrown up in the air and was now floating.

This is the deconstruction of your world that occurs when you are ready to leave it. When you are ready to transition, you see the physical world around you fall down. This is a good thing. It allows you to release your connections to the world. You felt it was bigger than you and controlled you but actually, it was your creation.

Your universe is yours to create on this side and the other. You can create it however you like. If you desire goodness, then you dream that into reality. You say to yourself, "I desire goodness around me. What does goodness look like, feel like, sound like?" Then you engage your senses and come up with an image in which the people around you are kind to you, you feel good about yourself, and you have positive self-talk in your head. You tell yourself, "I am loved. I am fine. Everything occurs kindly around me, and I enjoy my world." That is you creating your universe.

Question: So how do we create our home, or universe, on the other side?

When you decide to leave the universe you created for yourself in the physical realm, you must remove your attachment to those things you created so they can return to raw energy form.

This is the experience of dust to dust. When you, as spirit, feel you are complete and ready to move on, you erase from your reality what you had created so you can begin again.

Many individuals neglect to completely erase their world when they leave physical form. They leave energy structures around their creations that call them back. This is why you must call back any energy you have left behind when you transition. You must call back the forms you created, whether they are deposits of emotional energy, images, or sounds such as comments in your head. You must erase them from physical reality so you have your energy to create again on the other side or in another physical lifetime.

It is like having silly putty or clay that you use to create forms. You create a little house, a little dog, and a little you. You put everything that is appealing to you in the scene and then you begin the show. It is very entertaining. But when you are done, you need to gather up your silly putty and smash it back into an unidentifiable form so you can create anew.

You may say, "Oh, but in an unlimited universe where there is no lack, why is there a limit to my silly putty?"

And we say to you, "There is no limit, but there is a matter of cleaning up your act. There is a matter of calling your attention back to yourself. If your attention is left in previous experiences, you are no longer focused. As a creative being, you must focus to create. That is how it is done."

Chapter 4

People in the Room

You see, a multitude of beings are
pursuing the light at this time.

As Physsie began to make her decision to pass, she started having more dreams about friends and family members who had already crossed over. Some of these dreams were significant in that these people were obviously communicating with her through her dream state. They would come to her to see how she was doing and encourage her as she moved closer to her transition.

These dreams were frequent and vividly real. Physsie would tell us it seemed as if her friends and family were right there in the room with her when they were having these conversations. Often, she said they were telling her humorous things.

This contact became even more real when they showed up in Physsie's room while she was awake. She could see them and would let us know when her parents were there. She wanted me (Anne) to clairvoyantly communicate with them when she was having trouble understanding what they were saying.

Some of her friends would just show up and smile. This often brought Physsie to tears because she knew that they were there for her. She missed them and wanted them back in our physical world so she could talk with them again. But she was still thrilled to see them, even if she could not get them to say anything.

There is a fine line between imagination, hallucination, and psychic sight, which is why many people are quick to dismiss this extraordinary contact when, actually, it is real. Because we are psychics, we could see that Physsie wasn't crazy. Instead, she was seeing with her mind's eye exactly what was right in front of her, though it was appearing from a subtler density.

Sometimes people she did not know filled her bedroom and our house. This really concerned her because she had no idea what they were doing there. These were people who had died but were not aware enough to find the light and make it over by themselves. They were attracted to the light of Physsie's upcoming transition so we created a column of light for them to cross over and leave us in peace.

At other times, energies we referred to as "little gremlins" flew around the room. Later, we will talk more about these energies and the other topics that we only touch on briefly below.

Physsie had many friends during her lifetime, and most of them had already crossed over by the time she was ready to make her journey. Know that those you love, whether they are family members, friends, or animals, are there to support you in both your physical and subtler experiences.

Question: When Physsie was getting close to passing, there were many unseen energies in her room. Who were they and why did they come?

There were many friends from days gone by who came to check in on her and see that she was well. Her mother, father, and grandparents also showed up as supporters. They were there to tell her all would be fine. It was like a greeting team that arrived before she passed over.

There were also animals from days gone by, pets, and her totem animals, such as the bear. The bear was there to witness her transition. This was an honoring of her spirit, for she had loved bears, and they were returning the favor by protecting her as she crossed over to the other side.

Others in the room were simply energies that desired to control her. They were releasing from her system at that time and flying around the room. You call them gremlins, or negative elementals, that lack love and light. They were looking for a place to land because Physsie had decided to release them.

Beyond these individuals, animals, and energies, there were many in the room who came to assist her to the other side, like hospital staff at the ready in case she needed assistance. The staff were her completion team from the other side.

Also in the room were unseen individuals from the other side who desired to see how the transition was going and learn from it. You could think of these as professors or scientists who desired to see her progress and were curious to see how you helped her cross over. You and her support teams held her in love. This ability to hold the energy of love and bring in the light required a level of sophistication. Through their presence, these scientists also contributed to the success of this situation.

The drugs that were administered to her through hospice were meant to make her transition easier and more comfortable, rather than interfere with it. They were a form of assistance. Therefore, the completion team from the other side was monitoring the drugs in her system to ensure that they did not interfere with her spiritual growth. That was Physsie's desire. So the completion team monitored the administration of drugs on her behalf.

If she had instead said, "Please, get me to the other side. I don't care how I do it, just get me there!" then the completion team would have backed off and allowed the drugs to take hold more strongly. But Physsie desired to be aware during her transition, so she appreciated the minimization of the effects of the drugs on her spirit.

Question: At times, Physsie and Anne saw more beings than they could count wandering through the house. These were not beings we knew. Did other beings simply want to cross over with her?

Yes, there were those in your house at that time who desired to cross with the light of Physsie's transition. That is why we suggested putting a column of light in your backyard, which could help them cross, and instructing them to go there. By doing so, you assisted them in going to the light so they would no longer disturb you. You see, a multitude of beings are pursuing the light at this time. This is planet-wide. They have seen that ascension is possible and desire to move into the light but often are unsure how to do so themselves.

Chapter 5

Choosing When to Cross Over

There must be a desire to be present in this world to remain in the physical realm. Once you see the possibilities in the other realms, you can choose to go there.

Choosing when to cross over can be more complicated than you may think. The decision can involve other people and their events, so plans can be changed for a number of reasons. Physsie had fallen and could have easily died eleven months before she actually did. That is what the doctors expected. But she was given a choice to either enter a hospice facility in California or get well enough to fly home to Colorado and be under hospice care while living with us in our home. Her willpower kicked in because she had a reason to live longer. She was willing to do anything it took to come home to die.

To the amazement of hospice workers and volunteers, she was still walking around ten months later. But we felt she was preparing to go and were concerned that she might try to transition while we were out of town giving talks. So we asked Physsie's higher self if she could delay dying until we returned. This meant revising her plans, but her higher self agreed to wait.

At that time, we asked All That Is about her condition. The questions and answers below are presented in the present tense, just as they were asked and answered at that time.

Months Before Transitioning

Question: It seems like Physsie is moving to the other side even though she is adamant she wants to live a long time. What is happening?

Her personality is resisting moving to the other side. Her willpower is holding on. Through the direction of her higher self, her life force energy continues to pull out. As a personality, she keeps stomping her feet, demanding to stay. Her higher self is waiting because her personality is not done yet.

Ten Weeks Before Transitioning

Question: How soon is Physsie looking at passing? Can we ask her to delay it until we return so we don't put undue burden on the house sitter staying with Physsie?

It has occurred to her to pass while you are gone. She is looking at two to three weeks, at best, and this is that time frame. It would cause agony and discomfort for all concerned. She hereby agrees to pass after you return. It has been done.

Three Weeks Before Transitioning

Question: When is Physsie thinking of transitioning?

The personality known as Physsie is in transition at this time. She has seen her world disappearing. It is a world that no longer supports her being, so she has chosen to exit at this time. It may take days or weeks to complete the process of being fully present on the other side, but it has begun. The time frame is flexible. This process began for her months ago. There are still moments when she appreciates being in this world, and these moments continue the flow of life stream energy into her realm.

Two-and-a-Half Weeks Before Transitioning

Question: Anne woke up thinking Physsie had made her decision to transition last night after we did a healing with her. What happened?

The decision to transition has been made on a full body level now. Before, it was an etheric idea. It has now been settled. There is full determination to be on the other side. That decision was made last night during her sleep.

The healing you did with her yesterday allowed her to remember that she is God in charge of her realm and able to determine her outcomes. She feels she is no longer at the whim of others. She is creator of her universe, originator of her thoughts and being. This is her awakening.

Everything came together for her for this big decision. Synchronicities were created and everything fed into that experience of healing. You could say that her higher self was sitting by, watching, and you were instrumental in assisting her. She was given every opportunity to make her own decision. Everything fell into place and she decided to transition.

More than one thing happens at once. A conglomeration of things occurs. To assist her now, simply consider her as complete. Consider her as one who is whole.

Question: How did Physsie make that big decision last night?

Her whole being quit because it has had enough. She has seen enough of this reality and now feels hope for what is on the other side. She experienced reuniting with love there, and

47

she wanted to go. She physically felt love, which descended and let her know it was there for her. Physsie had the option to go and no longer felt the need to hold on to the physical realm.

There must be a desire to be present in this world to remain in the physical realm. Once you see the possibilities in the other realms, you can choose to go there. It is like saying to yourself, "I now have enough on my grocery list, so I will go to the store." Before you have enough on your list, there is less motivation to do so. But when you see your cupboard is bare you say, "Oh, I must make my way to the store now, whether I like it or not." That is how it works. Your motivation to transition increases and you make your journey to Source for cleansing and renewal.

Two Weeks Before Transitioning

Question: Last night I (Greg) dreamt Physsie was dying, but this morning she is very much alive. What is happening?

There is need to give relevance to the impact you have on another's being. Because you two are seeing yourselves as whole more often now, you are also able to see others, including Physsie, as whole. Last night, when you saw she was going, you saw her as whole. This influenced her not to go. That recognition of wholeness gave her the opportunity to choose again. She decided she could stay longer with that sense of wholeness about herself. She said, "I like the idea that I am whole," so she stayed. A new time line for passing showed up that she liked, so she switched to that time line.

It's like seeing guests to the door when they are preparing to leave your party. You say to them, "Hey, we just brought out the chocolate cake. Would you like a piece?" And they decide to remove their coats and remain. But moments before, they were headed out the door. That is how it works.

As for Physsie, her desire to continue remains and is fervently felt within her spirit, but her body is depleted. This conflict results in fluctuations in your time-space continuum or timeline, as you call it. Activities adjust accordingly, and her moment in time for release is adjusted. You see, you cannot assume you know the timing. You can pretend to know, you can assume you sort of know, but you cannot know wholeheartedly unless you are the only one involved. And that rarely happens.

Question: Did we do something wrong by influencing her to stay?

You simply let her see she had options, and she picked one. She may stay for a few days or a few weeks, but no more. This delay may be easier on you as well. You have some final completions to make, yourselves. You can give thanks.

Chapter 6

Completing and the Completion Team

*As one who is whole, you see no separation.
You see only love in the hearts of
those around you.*

What was left on Physsie's bucket list of things to do? We reviewed her list. Over the past few years, we had put photos in albums, done genealogical research, and made calls to friends and family. We had visited old family homes, family gravesites, and familiar places. We had eaten our favorite meals, resolved mysteries by finding items that had been lost for some time, and referenced the encyclopedia to answer nagging questions.

Physsie had also written her obituary and found a photo she liked to go along with it. She had updated her Christmas card list so I would know who to write when she passed. All these were acts of completion. We made Physsie's last week meaningful by talking, holding hands, and just being together.

As we were completing with her, All That Is brought to our attention that there was an unseen completion team working with her from the other side. We not only wanted to know what still needed to be completed, we also wanted to come to a better understanding of the completion team and their role. We asked these questions in that last week.

One Week before Transitioning

Question: Could you give us an update on Physsie's condition?

The one you call Physsie has passed. Most of her personality transitioned a few days ago. The entity with you now is what you call her higher self, the part of her that is wise and looks after her in life and on the other side.

It is mostly her heart you are experiencing now, not the personality. This is because her desire to complete is strong. She could not complete with her body experiencing so much pain. Therefore, the one you call Physsie left and the part of her that is whole, that can truly be love, is here now. You could say there was a split in energies, which is the result of the desire to be whole and complete. The part of her that could complete, her higher self, came forward with love.

Question: What does Physsie have left to complete?

She is releasing negativity from her system. She is purging the darkness within her. It is no longer necessary for you to hold on to her, for the majority of her is gone. The completion team, in the form of her higher self and some nonphysical assistants, are with her now. They are looking after her and completing for her the things she could not do for herself. This is a blessing.

Her desire to be complete has allowed for this. Otherwise, it would be a transition in darkness. She was encompassed by negativity and unable to escape its bounds—like a lion held in a cage. But by releasing the part of her that was her personality, by saying she was done and allowing others to assist, she allowed for the miraculous discovery that she had been whole from the beginning.

She, as a personality, had a misunderstanding that she was incomplete, even though she was complete all along. Once she realized this, the portion of her that recognizes wholeness in all things came forward to say good-bye and mean it. This is true love, for it encompasses all things. Those beings not in physical form who desire to remember and experience wholeness have come forward in support of this act. As a conglomeration of beings, they witness and hold space for this transitioning into the light. This is a group effort.

You may wonder how these unseen beings around her can be so supportive, and we say to you that within their core, it is in each person's nature to be whole. As one who is whole, you see no separation. You see only love in the hearts of those around you. This is the connection. You let go of the trappings, the negativity that holds you back, and you let yourself be love. This is the meaning of coming together and why they are here. This is why you incarnate over and over again and support each other. It is to experience this love within and around you.

Question: What is a completion team, and how did Physsie engage their services?

Physsie decided to pass over, so she began her transition. Her personality, or lower self, evacuated allowing her higher self to come forward and complete with you. It is time for her to be herself, her true self.

Physsie wants her transition to be easy on you. Therefore, she desired assistance and requested it. The completion team may be seen as an unseen emergency medical crew that comes in to assist with healing as requested. You can see them as orderlies and nurses dressed in white who attend to the details. It is a service that is available to all. There are a multitude of individuals who are ready to assist you when you ask for more love and light to be present in your system. They come forward. That is what is occurring.

Question: What do they clean up?

The completion team cleans up messes you have left behind. You could say that they prepare you to be moved out of your room to another area. To do that, they must unhook the tubes for mobility purposes. This allows you to be wheeled out of your room in an easy way rather than in an emergency fashion.

The team cleans up your body and comforts you emotionally. They remind you that you are the creator in your realm, that you created this transition, and that it is time for it. You who are preparing for this final transition lie in your bed and allow yourself to receive assistance. It is like requesting that a room be prepared for you on the other side, allowing others to prepare you for transport, and waiting for the receiving team on the other side to say that your room there is ready.

Physsie desired to have love surround her and support her as she prepared to cross. There are individuals who prefer not to receive assistance in their crossing, so they do not. They are more rugged in their demeanor and prefer to go it alone. Receiving assistance is all a matter of personal choice.

Question: Is the key to ask for assistance if you want it?

True, for you create on the physical plane and in the ether. Therefore, decide what you desire. If you focus on negativity in your transition, it will be yours. If you say, "I desire a completion team to assist me," they appear.

You may think that most people do not know what they want, but in their heart of hearts, they do. Physsie has been in the hospital many times before, and she knows how the system works. She remembers that experience and has relived that as a possibility. She does not want the negative side of it, but she does want the assistance, so she created it.

Question: Are angels and guides assisting her too? What can we do?

There are angels and guides in the room at this time. The completion team is there supporting Physsie in love. That is their purpose. The energy of support is given in all ways. As for what you can do, simply hold her in love. That love is all that is required— and requested—to maintain the energy field that allows light to come in during the time of transition.

Question: Is Physsie free now?

Yes, she is experiencing true freedom. She assumed the role of mother in this lifetime, but in reality, she is bigger than that. As she moves more completely to the other side, the dynamic of male and female is coming together within her. In the integration of spirit, there is no separation. This is true for all beings who desire wholeness. And for those beings who desire separation, they can have that experience.

Question: Previously, you said she was getting rid of the negativity. Is she still doing that now?

She is releasing negativity by letting it go and letting it be. She is not "getting rid" of negativity, for that would mean desiring its demise. This would cause more negativity to develop in her system. Physsie is saying, "Enough is enough. I choose to walk on." As she does so, the negativity releases itself from her system and floats away like dust in the wind. This will take a short time to complete.

Chapter 7

Events in the Final Days

The events were her own. You could not take that away from her. She was empowered by her choices and stood firm in her decision to pass.

The final days before Physsie passed, Greg slept in the chair in her room so he could be there to answer her questions and administer her pain medications. One night, after he had given her the 10:00 p.m. dose, he left the room to go write what he had done in her hospice log. She took that opportunity to get out of bed and follow him into the hall. But her legs would not support her and she fell towards him, crashing them to the floor together. As he propped her up on the floor, she angrily said, "You can't keep me here. Get Annie right now. She'll get to the bottom of this. She'll get me out of here. I need to go home."

At 3:00 a.m. the next night, after much conversation, Physsie finally asked Greg to turn out the lights because she was ready for sleep. He did this, and within minutes, she got up again to leave and find home. This time when she fell she crashed into the nightstand and shattered her shoulder beyond repair. According to the doctors and hospice, the only remedy for this was to give her pain medications. These helped her enter a coma-like state. No one could stop her from going home at that point. She made her crossing around 2:00 p.m. that Saturday, two-and-a half days later. On all levels, she orchestrated her exit beautifully.

These channelings were done the day after she crossed over.

Question: Physsie fell Tuesday evening but I, Greg, broke her fall, injuring myself. Did she want to die then?

She wanted to exit. This was one of her opportunities. When you broke her fall, it halted the process and altered her desire for the moment. She then completed with you the next morning by telling you she loved you, did she not? Holding your hand and kissing you on the forehead was her way of bringing in love for herself. This love allowed her to let go. She had blamed you for many things in her life, and this allowed her to let go of that negativity. By stopping her fall, you assisted her in seeing what she hadn't seen before, which was your open heart and your ongoing support of her. She became thankful.

Question: Physsie got out of bed and fell again early Thursday morning. Did she arrange it so I, Greg, couldn't catch her this time?

Yes, she was complete. By this next day, she had pulled out more and was not being affected by the negativity in her space. Then it was your (Greg's) negativity you had to deal with. You were angry with her for getting up and falling after you had cared for her all night. The negativity was releasing from you, so you could heal yourself with her passing.

**Question: But I feel bad about her falling.
Couldn't we have avoided that?**

The events were her own. You could not take that away from her. She was empowered by her choices and stood firm in her decision to pass. There could be no reversal at that point. The body was wasted, so to say.

Question: How did she decide it was finally time to die?

As dementia took over more completely in the last year, she was no longer herself because energies of negativity were running her life. Her willpower was diminished and she was less present in her physical form. On an energy level, she looked like Swiss cheese.

Before she came into this physical reality, she created a fail-safe device that would recognize it was time to go in case other energies took over her show or she forgot the agreement she had made before she entered her body. That arrangement made between her personality self, higher self, and full self was that she would return to spirit, or pass over, by her sixth or seventh opt-out point, no matter what she had or had not accomplished.

So when the time came to pass over and her personality was unable to make the choice to transition with awareness, her higher self had to push her along. It nudged her because it was a request she had made before entering physical form in this lifetime. Before she incarnated, she had said, "If I need assistance in the future from the wiser part of me to pass on, I want to receive that help at that time."

The result was that she got out of bed and fell, which moved her closer to transitioning. She allowed herself (her higher self), to help her (her lower self) without another, such as you, rescuing her. She also gave herself the reward of self-love by experiencing herself as whole. In the end, the negative energies that had taken over her system retreated because she and her higher self voided the contract with them when she saw how completely they had deceived her. She wanted to be herself again.

Question: When Physsie fell and crushed her shoulder on Thursday morning, they gave her medications to lessen her pain. What happened when she went into the coma-like state?

She rested. She had to release more toxins, or negativity, before she could leave. There was poison in her system from years of negativity that now needed to go. If she crossed over with negativity, it would cause her discomfort. Negativity is not of the world of love, so she had to detach from it. You could see it as her removing the sticky goo of negativity with rubbing alcohol. That is what she did. She passed a few hours after she was complete with cleaning out the negativity. She made sure she was clean first, and then she went.

Question: An hour before she passed and while still in a coma state, we explained that we would be busy for a while and that it was the day before the winter solstice, so the light would be returning soon. Even though she was in a coma, we wanted her to know everything so she could decide when to go. What effect did this conversation have on her?

It allowed her to release. Physsie liked the idea of being light on the other side as the light returned. She felt she was done and knew she had a window to leave while you were busy, so she took her opportunity to cross.

Chapter 8

The Transition Process

Transition from the physical to spirit involves deciding you are ready to go. You, as a whole being, must determine you are complete and it is time to move on.

The closer you are to a loved one, the harder it may be to accept that transition is near. You can see the signs, but sometimes you ignore them. Physsie started her transition years before she actually passed, and she explored the other side regularly through her dreams, which she shared with me (Anne).

Her back was visibly deteriorating and causing constant pain, her mind was becoming lost in dementia, and her faulty heart valve made her dizzy and nauseous most of the time. She was not happy about her physical condition even though she appeared to be cheery to friends. Her body was telling us she was getting ready to go, but her personality was determined to stay.

These channelings are a reflection back on the experience.

Question: How does the transition process work?

Transition from the physical to spirit involves deciding you are ready to go. You, as a whole being, must determine you are complete and it is time to move on. You may appreciate one aspect of your life but not feel complete in another.

For example, you may have completed the tasks you set out for yourself in your romantic relationships, yet you still feel insecure and unappreciated at work. You keep telling yourself, "I just need one more day to feel better. I really want to see others as whole." But upon arising each day, you forget that you are creator in your realm and that you created the circumstances in which you feel you are not in charge. You go to work and it happens again: your boss yells at you, you yell at others, and you feel incomplete and unloved. You are frustrated and overwhelmed by the need to control.

At some point, your higher self says, "I don't think this task is going to be completed in this lifetime," and your personality says, "No, wait. I've almost got it. I just need another day at work."

So the higher self stands back and waits patiently for the personality, the lower self, to run through more scenarios. But at some point, the higher self says, "We made progress, but the likelihood is that you will not experience enlightenment around this task unless you change something dramatically, and you are not desiring to change enough." The higher self sits back again and waits for the personality to become more exhausted. When this occurs, there is a decision to transition.

Leaving your physical body as spirit is a simple process. You do it when you sleep and dream. The journey at the end of life is no different from dreaming except that you disconnect from form and do not return. In the end, it is a matter of letting go. Some individuals are afraid to do this because they fear they cannot live without their physical form. They have focused mainly on the physical and not on the spirit. If you remember you are whole and feel more love in your heart for yourself, all will be fine. Know that you are God, creator in your realm, and you are able to create again. You are simply going back to the drawing board to draw out a new scenario in a new life.

Question: Could you explain the transition process from the perspective of the personality (or lower self), higher self, and spirit (or full self)?

At some point, enough is enough, and you are done with this life. Your spirit, or full self, the one who is in charge and knows all things, gives instructions down the chain from the subtle to the denser energies to release your physical form. Communications are made through your higher self. Your higher self is given the message from your full self that now is the time, and the one who has had the physical experience in form returns to the state of spirit without form. In this way, you regroup so you may return to physical form refreshed at another time.

Question: Could you explain it more?

Physsie's spirit, the part of her that is whole, decided it was time to pass. A message went from her whole self, or full self, down to her higher self, and the higher self relayed it to the lower self—her personality—that her time was up. When this occurred, most of the personality left the physical form and began its recuperation on the other side. This was the week or so before she physically passed. A minimal amount of the personality was left behind, and those particles of her being would be returned for recuperation when the body was laid to rest.

This is why you experienced more wisdom in her being that last week. You could say that her higher self took over the operations. She continued to release negativity, and during this time, anything left undone in the way of saying good-bye was completed. It was the desire of her full self to make amends, as necessary. When these communications were complete, the higher self was given the directive from the full self to pull the plug and return all energies to the other side for complete recuperation.

When the plug is pulled and the body is laid to rest, complete recuperation takes place. This is when another unseen completion team of so-called doctors and nurses appears and completes the transition on the other side. The higher self observes and watches over the lower self during this time. Remember, the higher self and personality are truly one unit, though they experience themselves as separate at this time.

The full self is aware of all things that occurred during that lifetime, and it begins to make an assessment of what is left to be done. It notices which personality traits might be improved. It also has complete awareness of all activities that have occurred in all lifetimes with all personalities. It takes those into account as well. A life review is made during which the personality, along with the wisdom of the higher self and the full self filtering through the higher self, view the situation. Decisions are made about what to do next. Others are involved in this process, but these are the main participants.

Question: What does Physsie have to say about her transition?

She wanted you to know that she desired to continue in life, but she knew she could not. Her physical body was failing. This required her to make an assessment of her situation. When she made her assessment, not all of her desired to go. But then she realized she could assist you in the task of creating this book from the other side, so she changed her mind and that allowed her to pass. Her commitment to assist you with this book brought her great joy, and that, combined with her previous commitment to opt out, took her to one hundred percent.

Physsie says, "Thank you so much. I truly appreciate the love you feel for me and hope you feel that love for yourselves. That is my hope for you. I hope you complete your tasks as I have done and that we move on together in love.

"Just so you know, I fell and hurt myself because it was my time to go. I wouldn't have gone otherwise because I was having too much fun with you to leave. It was a joy. You may not have seen it that way because I was difficult for you in the end, but it was. I really liked the idea of creating things with you and didn't want to stop. I want to continue doing great works."

PART TWO

Crossing Over
and Getting Situated

*When you get to the other side, it seems
no different from being in physical form.
You simply walk in your etheric body.*

When you leave your physical body for the last time, you transition from one reality to the next. You cross over from one realm of existence, which involves physical form, and enter a reality that is void of such dense matter. A healing environment then unfolds for you so you can choose to recuperate more completely and start enjoying the other side.

Crossing over and getting situated involves many activities of transitioning and recuperation. These activities can blend together and be fluid in nature. They can happen in an instant, depending on your level of spiritual development, or they can take a long time to complete. We have separated out these events to make them easier to understand.

Chapter 9

Making the Crossing

Your transition can be quite easy if your personality is willing to seek out the light.

Crossing over involves moving from one reality to the next. It is like going through a revolving door to move from a city street into a building. It is not a momentous occasion, but it is a transition. It is the same when you pass. You are in a physical reality and move to a purely etheric one.

The more aware you are, the more conscious you are of your options in crossing over. You may experience a simple tunnel of light that automatically takes you to the other side and the system of reincarnation. Or you may experience a string of light that unravels from your heart, which you follow to the other side. Alternatively, you may experience it as a portal that allows you to exit the reality you have lived in and move into another reality. With increased awareness, you will see more options available to you on the other side.

The reality that greets you on the other side of the tunnel is a design of your own beliefs or expectations. If you believe pearly gates are necessary to enter heaven and you think you are headed for heaven, then pearly gates will be there for you to walk through. These first images enable you to be more comfortable and accept your situation. Each crossing is unique and unfolds according to your level of awareness and your religious, cultural, and personal beliefs. You may focus on one aspect of the crossing and totally miss another.

Question: How would you describe the transitioning process?

This process can be described in a variety of ways. You could see it as a swirling ball of light, or white yarn, that encompasses your being as you prepare to exit your physical body and move into the purely etheric, or subtle, realm. You could also see yourself as entering a mist or cloudy area that allows other realities to unfold. This cloudy area—this energy system—exists for a few feet and blocks the vision of the previous reality as well as the reality to come, holding you as you transfer from one reality to the next.

Once you acknowledge and accept the ball of light or cloud that encompasses you, you can choose to step out of your physical reality and into a reality of your choosing. But until you have accepted this shift, you cannot make movement. It is like a brief pause that allows you a moment to acknowledge the shift, something like stepping onto an elevator and waiting a moment before you pick a floor and the door closes.

Question: When do you go through the tunnel of light? Does everyone go through a tunnel or do you have options?

When the time comes, your transition can be quite easy if your personality is willing to seek out the light. You can either look outside of yourself for answers or you can go within. You can see it as a tunnel or a string of light. You have options.

After you accept this shift in your reality, and while you are encompassed in this ball of light or cloud, you see in front of you a pattern of light particles that appear to you to be quite bright. Many interpret this as following the light ahead of you into a tunnel that calls you home. It has a sound to it that is quite familiar, like the Sirens calling to you in a Greek play. You follow this sound and light down what looks like a tunnel that opens up to a brighter light that encompasses you. This bright light can also be seen as a white mist.

In the second scenario, the scenario in which you go within, you seek the light within your heart by focusing on yourself as the one who created you. You see yourself as whole. You see yourself as everything at once. In this process, you could say that you choose to be more in charge of your crossing.

You can see this as a continuous string of light energy that emanates from your heart center and pulls you to the other side through the means of attraction. Your interest becomes fixated on this string of continuous light that unfolds from your heart and moves its way down what appears to be a round tunnel of swirling light in darkness. This is actually you exiting your physical form and becoming subtler in vibration as an energy being. You are simply watching yourself as light.

Question: Is this like going through a portal?

Yes, it is like a portal because it is the dissolution of one reality that gives rise to the recreation of another. You must have some method that tells your mind to be quiet and pay attention. Once you become quiet, you pay attention to loving yourself more as you transition. Then you pop out on the other side and are surrounded by love and loving beings.

You can see it as a portal because that is what it is. You can also see it as a tunnel created to assist you in your transition. At some level it is a contraption or creation of mind, but in its pure form, the tunnel is a portal that you create when you go within.

Question: What happens when you arrive on the other side?

After following this string or tunnel, you are encompassed by a bright light as you arrive on the other side. In this way, your spirit is returned to the light and your physical body is left behind. Out of this bright light come individuals who have loved you before and who hold you in admiration. They surround you and make you feel loved. At this time you may also notice that you are greeted by your higher self, that part of you that is wise. It is a homecoming—it is you returning to wholeness. You reintroduce yourself to yourself, to your guides, and to all those unseen advanced beings who have supported you and wished you well. It feels like you are seeing all those you love, for they surround you. And as you see them, you melt with the overwhelming experience of love, which allows you to relax.

Next, your creative mind calls forth images that are comforting to you. These images allow you to rest your mind and feel good about your choice to move ahead. If you did not desire to continue, you would not. You would return to your physical form and call this a near death experience.

You can say to yourself, "Oh, I desire to be in a realm of love with my loved ones," and you enter into that. You may say, "Oh, I desire to be around my old pets," and they appear. This is your created reality, which is permitted for a time. Eventually, you will be nudged to move beyond this, but for a time, it is meant to comfort you.

Question: So is this heaven?

Yes. Heaven is a resting place, or way station, where you appreciate yourself. It is developed on the other side to allow you time to recuperate. During your recuperation, you see loved ones around you. You feel whole, complete, and loved. Once you are on the other side, you breathe easier and experience simpler movements, more fluidity, less constraints. There is no real delineation between this life and the next. It is a continuation.

Question: How did Physsie get to the other side? Did she go through a tunnel or follow the string of light emanating from her heart?

What Physsie did was focus on the continuous string of light and not the tunnel. The tunnel could have been there for her, but she followed your coaching and chose to be more in charge of herself during her transition. You could say that she transitioned herself rather than having it done for her.

Physsie says, "I was with you and then I wasn't. I don't remember going through a tunnel. You told me not to. You said to look inside my own heart for the light, so I did. And that is where I found this jewel of brilliant golden light. This gem was me—it was my light. I followed this light inward and it got even brighter. The light came out of my heart and I followed it to the other side. It was really simple.

"Then I was standing in golden light, loving myself with other loving beings standing around me. I knew most of them, though not all of them intimately in the physical plane. They loved me and let me know it was all right. It was so beautiful. It was mesmerizing."

Physsie also describes it another way. She says it was as if she had received an evacuation notice. She followed the light on the floor as if she were a mouse following a piece of cheese attached to a curiously moving string. It moved across the floor of a tunnel-like area, attracting and pulling her to the other side. She followed this string and suddenly realized that she was in an all-encompassing bright light. The bright light held within it all the attributes of others she had loved. Images of beings she had known and appreciated appeared. They were there as reminders that she is a being of love.

This allowed her to settle into the idea that she is a subtle spirit. She had to accept this reality of bright light. Appreciating those she has loved allowed her to be present in this subtler reality of spirit. It allowed her to relax into love. As she did so, she became subtler herself. The images of love then dissipated, and she settled into being her subtle self.

Chapter 10

Recuperation

*Your recuperation is required in order
to participate fully on the other side.
Lack of wholeness, as a result of living
in physical form, must be repaired.*

Transitioning to a subtler density involves a period of adjustment and recuperation. After being in the physical realm, you need to rest for a while. The time it takes to rest and recuperate varies depending on your situation and the physical, mental, and emotional trauma you have endured. If you already released a lot of negativity from your system while you were alive, then your recuperation time on the other side can take less time than if you carry that negativity with you to the other side.

To fully release negativity, gather up all of your energy, and return to a state of wholeness at all levels of your being takes lifetimes and eons to complete. It is a healing process. You do what you can between lifetimes and within each life.

For quite a while, Physsie was aware that she was preparing to transition, and we talked about this freely. She intentionally addressed many personally challenging issues during her life.

The last two weeks before her passing, we did everything we could to help her release negativity so she might have an easier transition and faster recuperation on the other side.

Question: How does the recuperation process begin?

After transitioning through the tunnel or following the string of light, you are surrounded by loving beings. Those who have the task of tending to you as a newly transitioned spirit appear. Their presence allows the cleansing process to begin on the other side.

In a hospital-like setting, you are wrapped up, or cocooned, so that you remain still and do not harm yourself during recuperation. It is a "going inside" process. You sleep for a time, for you are gathering up your energies. You are calling yourself home. You are putting yourself back together as a spirit as you exit the physical realm. Many do not remember this process because it is done while you are partially asleep.

Question: Could you describe the recuperation process?

Your recuperation is required in order to participate fully on the other side. Lack of wholeness, as a result of living in physical form, must be repaired. Once your wholeness is repaired enough, you return from what you may consider to be a brief moment, even though it can take some time. Depending on your situation, you may stay in this place for moments, days, months, or years in Earth time.

The recuperation phase begins shortly after you cross over. You could view what happens as being met by a staff of loving caregivers who welcome you and take you to your hospital bed. They tend to your every need. Whatever you need to feel comfortable appears in front of you. At this time, you receive nourishment through light and love.

In this hospital-like setting, little is done mechanically except the administering of what could appear to be liquids if you arrive dehydrated, as so many do. In this case, the dehydration is really a lack of life force energy and flow. Life force energy is administered to you through what you would see as a drip sack of liquid, for this lets you know you are being cared for. It also lets you know it is time to reintroduce flow into your system so you can become strong again.

During this process, you also receive healing through the kindness of touch and light. Loving hands are placed on you, for example, through the wiping of your brow with a cool cloth. A hand may appear to check your pulse as well. Light, in the spectrum that is appropriate for you and your situation, shines on you.

You receive all the attention you need. You could see it as one caregiver or social worker per new arrival on the other side. Doctors and nurses come by as needed. The support staff is also available in emergencies. For example, if you arrive in a traumatized state, others are there to assist you in becoming calm.

This mental, emotional, and etheric (subtle body) recuperation continues until it is complete. If you accept that you are physically dead and feel ready to get on with your new life on the other side, then your recuperation can go quickly. But if you are severely mentally, emotionally, or physically wounded during your life or at the time of your death, your recuperation can take longer. This is because your wounds need to be healed to return you to wholeness so you can interact more fully on the other side.

You then have the ability to wake up out of this deep sleep and return to what you consider to be normal waking reality on the other side. This involves entering the world of beauty that is yours. You may call this heaven, and you feel at home. You may say to yourself, "Oh, I have been here before. I recognize this place." This is the resting place where you go between lifetimes. It is familiar to you, so there is a recognition process as you awaken from your deep sleep of recuperation.

Question: How does cocooning begin?

After the caregivers interview you and tend to your immediate needs, cocooning begins. Cocooning involves the intense healing that occurs when you are left to sleep for a time wrapped in what feels like a warm, soft blanket in your hospital bed. This recuperation process can take a while depending on how much negativity or contamination remains in your being when you cross over.

If there is little contamination, the cocooning can go smoothly and complete quickly. But if the contamination is thick—if you have attracted many other energies that have taken over your system—then remembering who you are can take a while. This is because the images that come forward through your creative mind are projected images that are not from you, the creator of your form. These images from others confuse and contaminate your being, and they must dissipate. For recuperation to occur, you must remember who you truly are.

And if many energies have projected images within your system, it can take eons to clear because a sorting out of realities must occur. Energies that are not the creator of the original being must exit, but they may not desire to do so. And you—the being who created the body, the being who had the original idea to create that form—may not desire to claim it. You may not want to accept your creation. But until some acceptance is made of creation, until acknowledgement is given, the cocooning process must continue.

This is the sorting process. You must say to yourself, "I created that body. That body is mine. I claim it and I love it." When you accept your form, then lack of form is accepted as well. The two merge and creation is able to be made again, which is the dissolving of one reality, or lifetime, allowing for the creation of the next.

Question: How did Physsie experience recuperation?

She says she experienced a softening. A cloudy material encompassed her and allowed her to rest. During this time she gathered up the parts of herself that were lost or fractured and brought them home to be with her in wholeness. This activity was attended to by others. Others saw to it that her threads of energy came forward to her so she could choose to incorporate them into her system—or not. If she chose not to recuperate fully, the threads would be allowed to remain unintegrated. There would be no recuperation in those areas that she chose not to heal. The opportunity was afforded to her to recuperate as she rested.

Physsie says, "You could see it as a platter being brought to you while you rest, and on this platter are the many parts of yourself that you left behind because of the issues you had with them when you died. You could say to yourself, 'I desire to incorporate this part within me again. I accept it now.' And with that, it is done. You can also say, 'I don't like that part. I don't want it,' and it disappears from the platter because you have chosen not to deal with it at this time."

That part would then need to be addressed at another time. For example, if you don't want to see yourself as a bully because you dislike bullies, then the part of you that is a bully would be left behind in the configuration of your personality to be addressed later.

Question: Could you review what it was like for Physsie shortly after she passed?

Originally, Physsie was thrilled to be on the other side. But then she realized she wasn't with you, and it caused some deterioration in her system. She went under recuperation at that time, healing in her own way. She separated herself from loss and disappointment and saw herself as whole.

Given she did not see herself as whole for so long, it required the attention of others to devise a system to make her feel loved during this process. A staff of doctors and nurses surrounded her at her bedside, allowing her to release toxins from her system so she could continue. She was willing to do so and submitted herself to the process.

If she had been unwilling to participate, the process would have been less attended to at that time. She would have been allowed to rest on her own. But her desire to grow attracted the attention of these doctors and nurses. They adjusted the subtle systems that maintained her existence as she released more negativity. They attended to her as you would to someone who needs to be watched closely because her energy system had been on the edge of a breakthrough. And to achieve this, there had to be subtle adjustments that were accepted by her and administered by others to whom she had given permission.

Physsie asked for growth and expansion, even though her desire had been to remain with you, alive in her physical body. She did not fully desire to go to the other side. However, her higher self, through her full self's urgings, came to the decision that it was necessary for her to transition, given her prior agreements. Any further delay would have caused damage not only to her, but to the two of you as well. Exhaustion from dealing with negativity was too draining for all of you.

So with the desire for growth, a decision was made for Physsie to ascend to the other side. Ascension is the returning of subtle energies, or higher vibrations, to your system, which allows you to grow. Ascension is not a magical process. It is a necessary process to shift dimensions, or densities.

Question: *Anne had a relative who was alcoholic and often angry. When he died, she clairvoyantly saw him being cocooned for many years. Could you explain his healing process?*

Through the cocooning, he was altering his being to detoxify himself. That required time. It also required rest. This is typical of situations where you abdicate, allowing other energies to rule your world. There is a lessening of your strength, which requires extra attention and rest on the other side so you can return whole. It may take eons if you have lost yourself so much. But all people return to wholeness at some time.

There are some individuals who, during the healing process, awaken enough and decide to escape out of their cocoons and return to "the land of the living," or physical reality. You would consider these individuals to be discarnate entities. They have chosen to forgo the reincarnation process and swing back into the physical realm without a new body for themselves. We suggest that this is not a desirable way of doing things, for they are without wholeness.

It is best to remain in that cocoon, or hospital bed, until you are more loving of yourself. But this is a challenge at times because there have been so many other energies running through you that you have forgotten that you are God, the creator in your realm. This situation requires more growth and attention during recuperation. If you are unwilling to receive that attention, there is nothing the energies of light can do. You have free will, so you may remain in darkness for some time.

Question: Anne's father was also alcoholic and angry much of his life. When he died, she clairvoyantly saw that he did not cocoon as long. What was the difference?

He was accepting of more light. When he died, you (Anne) and your sister held him in light. You intentionally asked for his self-forgiveness and the release of his spirit. You were not messing around. You meant it. And your father meant it too. He desired growth and acceptance at that time, which released his spirit from the negativity that had held him for so long. This lessoned the healing process on the other side. You could see it as the releasing of negativity through choice.

Question: We had a more consciously aware client die recently, and Anne clairvoyantly watched as she entered recuperation. She seemed to consciously participate in the whole process. How was that?

She asked for self-forgiveness and self-acceptance immediately. She knew she could no longer continue with negativity. She had done great work healing herself while she was alive, so there was little to be done on the other side. She was aware of her choices and chose to participate with more awareness. You watched her sit on her hospital bed communicating with her social worker so she could fully understand the process before her recuperation began. This was good and somewhat unusual. She wanted to grow in her wisdom and witness her own healing process.

Chapter 11

Your Higher Self and Recuperation

When you become a more integrated being while in the physical, you have less need for recuperation when you die.

Your higher self and your lower self have different needs. Your lower self needs to recuperate while your higher self remains in the light, supporting your lower self in any way it can. The more your higher and lower selves are integrated during your lifetime by loving and accepting your body, mind, and emotions, the less time will be required in recuperation. Ultimately, your higher and lower selves are meant to reunite as one in your experiences.

Question: What does your higher self do while your lower self is recuperating and cocooning?

When you transition out of your physical body and take only your subtle body with you to the other side, your higher self is available to receive light from Source. During this time, your individual personality, or lower self, recuperates. This involves repairing the aspects that have felt wounded during a lifetime, and it includes the hospital stay and cocooning for a time. In this way, you rest and receive nourishment while the higher aspect of you receives light.

The needs of these two parts of you differ. The lower self has experienced much. It is like someone who has been on a journey and has come home dirty with scratches and wounds. These physical, emotional, and mental wounds must be tended to.

Tears in the etheric body, which corresponds to the physical body, must be repaired to return you to wholeness. Emotional wounds, which involve attachments to individuals and events, must be repaired by calling back your energies and removing energies that belong to others. This allows your emotions to return to a state of balance. As for mental wounding, thoughts you have had about yourself that were unkind must be released so you can see clearly again. This all takes place during what you call healing, or cocooning.

While these parts of you are being repaired, your higher self—that part of you that is wise and that has remained in the light—continues to be in the light. The wounding occurs at the lower levels of experience, not at the higher level of self. When you communicate with one who has passed, you can speak with either the lower or the higher self. You simply must ask. These communications will render different information and images.

Question: When people initially pass, Anne often clairvoyantly sees them as younger, healthier, and at a distance. Is she seeing images of their higher selves?

Yes. She is seeing the higher self, separate and yet still whole. The lower self has gone out, had experiences, and returned. This is when the lower self rests and heals. During this time, you often see the images as quite different from the individual you knew right before she crossed over. You can always ask to see an image of either the higher self or the lower self. It is your option. If you don't specify your desire, you will be shown the one that is most familiar to you, which is the lower self, the personality. Once the lower self has recuperated, it will appear more like the higher self because it has come closer to wholeness.

Anne relates this story, which might explain it further. "Years ago, I (Anne) asked to communicate with my grandmother (Physsie's mother), right after she passed. I was immediately shown the image of my grandmother as younger, driving over grassy hills and stopping at gas stations along the way to fuel up. The light was diffuse yet bright and everything was beautiful. When I tried to catch up, she quickly made her way to the next gas station on the next knoll. I interpreted this as my grandmother showing me the image of her higher self doing well in the sunshine, accepting light, while her lower self received fuel during her healing process. My grandmother was truly fueling up, in many regards.

"When Physsie passed, I also clairvoyantly saw her at a distance, held in light, looking younger and serene. I assumed that I was seeing Physsie's higher self. She was not personally involved with me, but she was available to me. There was little personality that I could detect in that image. I was witnessing more of her pure self, or the pure essence of her being. I assumed that her personality self was going through repairs and recuperation."

Question: When you are more consciously aware and have integrated your lower and higher selves more, what happens during recuperation?

When you become a more integrated being while in the physical, you have less need for recuperation when you die. You tend to your wounds as you go through life and do not leave them hanging out there for a time. Instead, you are aware of what you have done. "Oh, I made a mistake in judgment. I held a mistaken assumption and my emotions went awry. I mistakenly abused my physical body because I did not realize it could not handle so much stress." When you realize these things, you apologize, forgive yourself, and love yourself back to wholeness. When this occurs, the wounding disappears and a pure state of love brings about healing.

When you get to the other side, it seems no different from being in physical form. You simply walk in your etheric body. You are like a car that drives on land but can also transform into a boat and float on water. You start out in a physical form, and then you shift into a subtler form, which is quite natural. The wounding is what is unnatural because it is a lessening of your light. When the light returns, you are able to move through worlds with ease. That is your natural state.

Chapter 12

The Fracturing of Energy

At your core, you are whole, but by fracturing yourself, you have forgotten your wholeness.

Have you ever been talking to someone while your mind was a million miles away, thinking about something else? Have you ever looked at an old photo and felt like you were back in that experience? This is fracturing, splitting, or splintering your attention and energy. Now imagine this happening not only throughout your life but also over lifetimes. To return to wholeness, you must reincorporate these parts of yourself. Your wholeness must become the center of your attention.

This fracturing mostly happens on an unconscious level. By bringing it to your awareness, you can intentionally choose to call yourself back to the present. There is no need to know exactly what you are calling back as long as you intend to return yourself to wholeness.

The first step in returning these fractured parts is to realize that they are out there. The next step is to choose to call them back as many parts as possible during your lifetime. Finally, you call back as many remaining parts as you can after you cross over during the process of energy retrieval. The total process of returning fractured parts is ongoing throughout your existence as a full self.

Question: *Are you supposed to call back your energy from everything, such as people, places, things, events, thoughts, and other realities?*

Yes, you are. It is the fracturing of yourself that you are repairing by returning energy to Source through your higher self. This is your return to wholeness. At your core, you are whole, but by fracturing yourself, you have forgotten your wholeness.

Question: *Is that why recuperation includes calling back your energy?*

True. If you were to call back your energy in the present moment and not leave portions of yourself in other places in time, then you would have all your energy with you. There would be no need to call it back during recuperation on the other side. But the recuperation process is not complete until your energies have been called back.

When you are in physical form, there is no leakage if you say to yourself, "I can maintain my energy system. I keep my energy to myself because it is a part of my system, and I feel blessed by it." There is no depositing of your energy in other spaces and times. Depositing occurs when you fracture yourself. When you are whole, you maintain your energy system fully and it flows evenly. You have ideas and from these ideas, you create easily and well without any disruption in yourself. When you fracture, you are disrupted and no longer whole.

Question: *Are incarnations really the fracturing of your full self's thoughts into other places and times?*

True, very much so. Every time you, as a full self, have a thought, it is you fracturing off a part of yourself into a reality you design for yourself. That incarnation is a thought you have of yourself. Your higher self manages and maintains you as a lower self in that incarnation.

If you, as a personality, think of yourself as sitting on a beach while your body is actually sitting in a chair at home, you are splintering off a part yourself and incarnating it on that beach. There are now two experiences of you going on simultaneously. Each time you look at an old picture of yourself and imagine yourself in that old experience, you are splintering yourself off. You must call these energies back to be whole.

You have thousands upon thousands of incarnations of yourself in your world at one time. That is why you must call those energies back. This is not an impossible task because when you truly desire yourself to be present, you are. You remind yourself that each time you desire to be someplace else, you take yourself there, and you simply choose to bring yourself back and be more fully present in the moment.

Being present is important. Most people lack being present. If you look at perpetual daydreamers, for example, they have trouble listening to what you have to say because their attention is somewhere else. If they brought themselves to the present moment, they would be able to listen and all would be fine. But when you leave a portion of yourself in a reality, your ability to be present in the current reality diminishes and you become less functional.

Question: How does the higher self manage thousands and thousands of incarnations, or fracturings?

You, as a being, are multi-dimensional. You have many experiences of form in time and space, and these are multidimensional. This is why there are thousands upon thousands of them.

These ideas of yourself are managed through your higher self. They are all experiences of who you are. They have splintered off as you have had more ideas about yourself. For you to fully recuperate, you must gather up your energy and bring it back to Source through your higher self.

Your system is allowed into being through the love of the higher realms. Love is your containment field. You must focus on calling back your energies to simplify your world and create your desires. When you are so fractured, you cannot create, for a sufficient amount of energy is required to create what you want. Whether you call yourself back in this lifetime or the life thereafter is immaterial. It must be done at some point if you desire to return to Source and experience yourself as a full and whole being.

Question: Does each thought you have create a splintering?

True, very much so. That is you going out into the world, into the realm of experience. But when you desire to return home to the light, then those parts of you are sucked back up into yourself. This is the coming home experience. This is returning to the light. This is eliminating the fracturing through the desire to have your parts reintegrated into yourself.

Question: How do you call yourself back if you are constantly having new thoughts?

You could see this as a process that rolls forward, like waves in an ocean, as you have thoughts. You gather up the thoughts you have completed, and then you think new thoughts that go out into your world to create. You continuously roll forward onto the shore with new thoughts as you gather strength from past thoughts returning to you as full self—Source, the ocean.

All you need to consider is that you are calling yourself back. You are loving yourself into wholeness. That is the focus. Once you do this, there is more energy available for you to create anew. Until you call back your energy, you do not have enough of you to produce new experiences because you have distributed your energy far and wide. But when you gather up your energy, you can move ahead.

Chapter 13

Energy Retrieval

The lower self must locate all areas where it has left itself in places and times so it can gather itself as a whole for its review.

W hen you interact with anyone or anything, you can knowingly or unknowingly mingle your energies, taking on their energy and giving them yours. Your aura can end up looking cloudy instead of clean. Collecting the energies of others in your aura can weigh you down. And if you have given away your energy through fracturing, your energy and strength can be diminished.

For many years, Physsie had been practicing techniques that we teach about grounding, calling back your energy, setting your energy space, and clearing out your energy system. But due to dementia in her final years, she was rarely grounded. Her attention and energy were scattered and her space was overcome by energies that were not her own. However, during her last week, her higher self took charge, and she was able to make huge progress in calling back her energy. She was also able to clearly see the energies of others in her space and ask them to leave. She did this work while she was awake and asleep.

Energy retrieval is intended to be a continuous process for us as energy beings. You can call back your energy and clear your space at any time before you transition. If you are not aware that you can do this, you do it all after you arrive on the other side during your recuperation in the hospital-like setting.

Question: What did Physsie notice about the calling your energy back process?

She says it was like being in the center of a whirlwind where you cannot move. These energies were quite swift. There was little she could do to shift her attention because she was held in a place that was small and contained. She says it was like being in a stadium seat with people seated around you. You cannot get up and move around.

Physsie says, "I was aware I was contained. It was happening to me, even though I was the center of the process." She says it was like being put in an egg-shaped containment field that was activated, and she had nothing to do with it.

Question: Can Physsie more fully describe the process of gathering up her energy on the other side?

Physsie says that she was in a bit of a daze before this process. Then it felt like she went to sleep and had a dream in which she experienced a whirlwind around her and something was being done within her awareness but not according to her conscious efforts. This whirlwind took her from realm to realm, gathering up her energies. It was like taking a journey through space and time to find herself. Once her pieces were gathered up, she became able to focus on herself. She says she just woke up having to regroup and figure out where she was. To her, this process was quite quick. But in actuality, her overall recuperation took closer to six months in physical time.

Question: Did her personality and her higher self go through this whirlwind together?

The whirlwind is what happened to her personality. Her higher self was quite calm and beyond this, receiving light. It was already experiencing the other realms while the details of gathering up energy were being tended to. Her higher self was not involved with the time-space physical experience, so it did not need to tend to the time-space cleanup. In other words, if you are not part of a situation, it is not your responsibility to deal with it. You might say, "Oh, but her higher self was in this world." And truly, it was, through her personality. But it was mainly her personality who made the decision to incarnate. Her higher self did not need to have another experience. It was simply there as a guide for her as she had this experience to grow. Therefore, it was the lower self, the part that incarnated, that had to clean up after itself.

Each part of you is responsible for different things. The lower self that incarnates is responsible for that incarnation. It is allowed to act freely through free will and, therefore, must tend to itself. The higher self is there to assist the lower self in gaining understanding and wisdom about how to maneuver well through this world. But it is ultimately the responsibility of the lower self to clean up after its incarnation. Therefore, the lower self must locate all areas where it has left itself in places and times so it can gather itself as a whole for its review.

In this life review, the lower self can gain understanding about where it might choose to go next. It can also choose to remain on the other side for a time as one who assists or guides those on the physical plane. That is what Physsie is choosing to do at this time. She is choosing to set up shop as one who assists you as you write this book. That is her goal and job. Others may choose to incarnate quickly. She says she has no need for that at this time. Her setup on the other side is all she requires to move ahead now.

Question: Was Physsie aware of others in whirlwinds gathering up their energies?

This whirlwind activity is personal. It occurs for each individual. Individuals are not privy to the material that is gathered by another because that is private information. Within each whirlwind, you focus on yourself. That is the point, for most have been outwardly focused for so long that much energy must be gathered.

Physsie says, "When I looked around, I could see a lot of individual whirlwinds or egg-like devices that I assume had individuals inside of them. From the outside, they looked like fuzzy, cottony, grayish-white masses. But from the inside of my own whirlwind, it looked like things were twirling around me."

Question: Beyond Physsie, we know Lewis Bostwick on the other side. He is advanced in his awareness and developed psychic energy techniques that we teach today, which are similar to the ones you are describing. Did he go through this whirlwind phase when he died?

Lewis says he saw the whirling of a light device coming towards him and chose to move aside. He says, "I desired to call back my energy through a more conscious approach. So I chose to appreciate myself in my multiple forms and allow those parts to become more of a conscious part of me."

This is one way of doing it. It is an option for everyone, though doing it yourself is used less and less these days. Most feel the calling back of energy through external devices is done more easily. They appreciate that and step away from doing it themselves. And most individuals need assistance. The whirling Physsie experienced was done to her. She entered the device to call her energy back. But there are more possibilities available to you.

Question: Lewis, would you say that the whirlwind device is a bad thing?

Lewis says, "No. It is a contraption that has been devised for those who desire assistance. Through time, it became a device that people came to rely upon. I desire not to be dependent upon devices. Therefore, I choose to do it alone. But there are many options available to you when you return to the so-called 'other side.' Most individuals cannot find the energy within themselves to do this process alone. That is why the device was originally constructed. You could say that it has an unconscious aspect to it because it is a contraption, or configuration of energy, that is designed for you rather than being purely you. It is not bad. It is good for those individuals who need assistance, and most individuals fall into that category."

Question: All That Is, how do you suggest calling back your energy while you are still alive?

You call your energy back through the desire to do so. You say to yourself, "How can I be more present today? I had a thought yesterday that I was on a resort island, but I live in a city. I know I took a part of me and deposited it there with that thought, so that part of me is not available to me now. I desire to bring back that part of me from my mental vacation."

Then feel yourself being fully whole and present where you are now. Appreciate and enjoy your current situation. You call back your energy through enjoyment because you must be present to enjoy yourself. Laugh at yourself and your situation because laughter brings to you a vibration that reverberates throughout your being and calls you home. It ripples through your system. It is a sound that calls you home.

Question: Is it the intention to be whole that calls back your energy?

True, very much so. Intention is your desire to be a certain way. It defines who you are. It is the defining of desire that allows for the creation of your desires in form.

Intention, or intense desire to be whole, along with the love of self, recalls your energy. The intention is you being the creative spark of light, which you are. The love of self is you appreciating who you are. These two ingredients are required to call back your energy and be whole.

Chapter 14

Touring the Other Side

It looks like a crystal city. Everything is pure, clear, and clean, and there is a place for you there.

What you experience on the other side depends on your level of awareness. If you believe heaven is supposed to look a certain way, then you create that image, that reality. Within reason, your beliefs and desires create your reality. It all depends on your awareness and what you are open to experiencing. It is the same in heaven as it is on Earth.

Physsie wanted to be loved and supported on the other side, so she created a loving environment with other people. She wanted to know things, so a crystal city with places where she could learn and grow appeared before her. She created her reality with every thought.

Question: Physsie, what was it like to become more aware on the other side after your recuperation period?

Physsie says, "For me, after I recuperated it was like walking through a door and moving through a cloudy room. You are not sure where you are for a while because it is like just waking up. Then you emerge into what looks like a beautiful valley. You look around. It is natural with fields of grass and flowers and trees in the distance. You ask yourself, 'Where am I? What am I doing here? Am I in a dream?' And then you walk further and notice that the dream continues. It feels like you are in a land that is beautiful yet strangely different. There appear to be no people, and it is calm, safe, and secure. You stay there for a while to become acclimated to the beauty. This goes on for a time."

Question: What about the people there?

Physsie says, "After you become acclimated, people start emerging from the distance and come towards you. It is like old friends week. They talk telepathically and shine with love, glad to see you and glad that you have arrived. They reach forward to touch you and tell you that everything will occur in good timing and that you should be concerned about nothing. Just be glad you are there. They tell you that you are fine.

"They gather around you and make you feel good inside. It is that loving warmth that surrounds you. You feel like you never want to leave this time. But then there is a channel that opens in front of you. It is as if the crowd parts and there is a space that is maybe ten people wide now available for you to walk ahead into the city.

"This is when you are shown that there are buildings, which were not evident before. It looks like a crystal city. Everything is pure, clear, and clean, and there is a place for you there. You walk ahead knowing that you can enter any of these buildings at any time through your desire to do so. But you are told not to enter until it is the proper timing. I do not understand what 'the proper timing' is, so I allow others to be in charge of telling me when I may enter."

Question: Physsie, can you describe the buildings? What is your focus over there?

Physsie says, "You make your way through natural scenery to what appears to be a city of crystal palaces that awaits you for learning and discovering about yourself. These buildings look like ice structures, but they are not cold. One of these buildings, which looks a bit like a cathedral, has all of the memories housed within it of my past and everyone else's past as well. They call it The Hall of Records. It is where I go to look things up and find the locations and experiences of old friends. It has books and an old card catalog system that I go through. I have been there many times since I arrived.

"I want to know everything about old friends, but I am not involved in their relationships. I allow them to have their experiences and I don't interfere. They have their own families that they are concerned about, or I should say not concerned about because there seems to be no worrying here. But they are focused on certain relationships, and I acknowledge and respect that. I look them up to see what they are doing because that might give me more ideas of what I want to do myself.

"My focus is on loving me. I had not done that in so long that I forgot what it was like to be the center of my own attention. So that is my focus. I am not tending to another. I am not assisting another in recuperation as many are doing. Some grandparents are looking after their grandchildren in physical reality. I am not. I feel it is time to look after me, and I simply consider my grandchildren to be in charge of themselves.

"It is also a priority for me to focus on myself. That was missing in my last life. I focused so much on others that I forgot who I was. I want to recuperate and remember myself. It's not that I am bad or wrong, and I know that now. But I was a bit off target in considering everyone else before myself. I truly lost myself, and that is what I must find now. That is my recuperation. It involves returning to wholeness, and that is where I must begin."

Question: Are there animals there? Do you take classes?

Physsie says, "I see dogs in the area. They are available for those who want to receive love from them or give love to them. But they are not my focus at this time. I became lost in animals, as well as in other people, when I was alive. So I must refrain from doing that in this lifetime, in this reality here, and be more focused on myself. I must find ways to entertain myself without relying on others.

"I have been here for a time now. I have learned that there are many classes being given on any topic you desire. You simply have a desire to learn something and then a teacher and a small classroom appears. You may be the only student or many people may be interested in the topic and the classroom is then more of a lecture hall with seating that goes all the way up to the ceiling. The size of the classroom depends on the interest level in the subject.

"There is also a grand hall with all the choices you have for learning. You can go in one door, sit down, and learn in one area and then leave that place and go in another door, sit down, and learn in another. You have the right to continue with a class or leave and go to another. You eventually desire to be on your own and create. That is when you put out the desire to know how to do so."

Question: Physsie, where are you sleeping? How do you make yourself comfortable?

Physsie says, "I'm sleeping on the floor in the hallway of a large marble-like hall where people go to take classes in the daytime. There is really no one there at night. I don't want to get too attached to this place called heaven, so I haven't identified a separate place for myself. I might need to go somewhere else, so I want to be mobile.

"But I guess I could have a bed or a couch to sleep on that could go up against the wall. That would be quite comfortable, and no one would complain about that. Actually, I could create a little house for myself. Why don't I do that? That's a good idea! That would be even better. I'll make it really close to the classrooms so I don't have to walk too far. I'm taking classes now and I don't want to miss out. I forgot I can create these things and create them again if I move. It is up to me. I have to remember that."

Question: What about eating over there?

"All you have to do is desire to go to lunch and suddenly there is a lunch hall in front of you that looks like the one in *Harry Potter* but without the drama or fanfare. Actually, the one I'm describing looks more like a big summer camp dining hall, but with taller ceilings. There can be any food you like in this cafeteria. Whatever you desire appears.

"The difference is you don't feel so addicted to food. You desire broccoli casserole and there it is. You put it on your plate, and doing that is practically the completion. You eat it and experience it, but that doesn't seem to be the focus. The focus is more that you desired to be in the cafeteria and have broccoli casserole. You sit down and say to yourself, 'Now I have it, and now I am complete.' You don't actually have to eat it.

"Every desire completes and there's no lack, so there's no yearning. You don't need to eat vanilla ice cream over and over again to feel satisfied. You look at it and think to yourself how nice it is to have vanilla ice cream. That is all. And then you move on and think of something else. If you think it would be nice to see a yellow bird, one appears, you recognize how nice it is to see it, and then you move on."

Question: All That Is, could you explain addiction on the other side?

Once recuperation is complete and you are fully yourself, there is no attachment to anything that is impure, which is the experience of lack. There is no attachment to lack because everything you think of is available to you once you desire it. If you desire to see an old friend, the old friend appears and you are not missing that old friend. The goal is to be complete. As you recuperate, you become less and less attached and more and more yourself.

If an old professor of yours is near and dear to your heart, you simply request that he appear, and he is there for you, completely. He looks in your eyes and is present with you. You do not have to gain his attention through chatting. He simply looks at you, you look at him, and all is known. You do not have to ask questions either, for there is no lack of understanding. Again, all is known. You could say that this desire to see someone arises from lack, for you feel somewhat incomplete in that relationship. But when your professor appears, you look at him and you are complete. It is like putting ice cream on your plate. You wanted ice cream, you requested it, and your request is fulfilled. Your desire dissipates.

Physsie wants to add something. She says, "This ability to create what you want takes some getting used to. I used to be concerned that I would not get enough vanilla ice cream, but whenever I have a little yearning for ice cream or remember how much I wanted it when I was alive, I am reminded that everyone around me loves me. No one hates me here. No one tells me I can't have something I want. Everything I want I have immediately, so I relax. This is a very supportive place.

"I do want to explain, though, that I miss being with you. But whenever I have that thought, I am told that I'm surrounded by love and that I can let go of those old ideas of not having enough. This is part of my growth, and I'm getting better now."

Chapter 15

Seeing Family and Friends

You see whomever you like on the other side.
Your desire creates your loved ones in
front of you.

Physsie had many old friends she talked to regularly by phone. When they passed away, she cried and added their death days to her birthday calendar so she would continue to think of them. Beyond editing our materials, these connections and phone calls were Physsie's focus. In those last years, she had an overwhelming desire to connect with loved ones on the other side. She regularly asked us to check in with them clairvoyantly so she could know how they were doing and let them know she cared. We expected her to be consumed with friends once she passed over.

Question: What is it like to see family and friends on the other side?

Your experience of seeing loved ones differs depending upon your level of awareness. When you desire to see loved ones, they appear. But you realize their appearance is of your own making, so you attribute less significance to them. You say to yourself,

"I am a loving being. I am surrounded by love," and you create within yourself and your universe the experience of love because you are in charge.

If you are not in love with yourself enough yet and it feels incomplete when you say, "I am surrounded by love," then you feel lack. When you desire another's love to fill you, you yearn for the experience of being surrounded by love because you have not filled yourself, so you create loved ones around you to fill that emptiness.

Your experience on the other side is dependent upon the amount of love you have for yourself. To feel no lack, you must love yourself enough to accept yourself as God, creator in your realm. So filling yourself with love is a goal during your life, during your stay on the other side, and during your next life.

Physsie loved herself more when she passed. She says, "Your family and friends are there, but it's not the same. Friends are good, and you love them very much, but you also must have something you do for yourself. When I was alive, I had a good thing going when I edited Annie and Greg's materials, and I want to continue that from here. That is my plan."

Question: Are there spiritual families on the other side?

No, not exactly. From a higher perspective, that assumes exclusion. If you have a family, then you have those who are not in your family. Instead, we would say that there are those with whom you affiliate because you are likeminded. This is a natural gravitation where like vibrations gather in natural groupings, and over time, the group shifts—not dramatically and not often, but groups can reconfigure. It is like looking through a kaleidoscope over time, or more specifically, over experiences. Some naturally gravitate to one direction and some gravitate to another. As you become more likeminded, you feel more affiliation to the kaleidoscope crystals around you. But you do not divorce one family and join another. It is more of a natural reconfiguration.

Question: Has Physsie seen her friends much on the other side? She was so looking forward to their reunion.

She says, "Of course. They are all around me. They were here for me, surrounding me with love as I entered heaven. But now they are doing their own things. Most of them are not trying to discover who they are, as I am."

For Physsie, seeing them on her arrival was a complete experience. Because of that completion, she felt satisfied, and out of that completion came an awareness of where she was incomplete in herself. She understood that she must fill herself with love rather than rely on others to fill her. With this experience, she realized that she must find her way home to herself rather than follow others to their homes, and she decided to take up this task.

Question: Has Physsie seen much of her first husband, Beach, the love of her life who died when she was thirty? She never stopped missing him when she was alive.

Physsie says, "I saw him here, and he was fine. There were a variety of women hanging around him, and he was more confident with them than when I knew him. I now feel that connection is complete, and I have a warm and fuzzy feeling about it. I have no need for romance beyond that.

"You can be incomplete and then complete things in a moment. I completed my journey when I saw Beach again. It was like old home week. Once I found him and it was complete,

I reveled in that for a time, and then I started wondering what more there was for me to do. What was left undone in my lifetime, beyond seeing Beach again? I considered taking care of myself and finding a way that was right for me alone. I realized that was where I was incomplete. I had completed love by feeling satisfied with Beach, but I had not finished determining what was right for me alone. So that is what I must discover. Who am I outside of a relationship and outside of reacting to the circumstances around me? I have not determined that yet, so that is my quest."

Question: Who can you see on the other side? We thought Physsie's first husband would have reincarnated by now and not fully be there.

You see whomever you like on the other side. Your desire creates your loved ones in front of you. If you want to see your first husband, you can even if he has reincarnated. It is no different from desiring to create a widget in your world. You say to yourself, "I desire to create a widget. How shall I do this?" You bring your widget into form through creating it. You may say, "Oh, but I had my widget constructed at a factory." And we say to you, that is one way of doing things. Another is simply to have your desire create through your imagination, and this internal construction of an event brings forward your desired experience. Everything is created through your desire to have an experience. This is the setup in your world on both sides.

Question: Can you explain creating some more?

All things you desire, as an individual or as a collective, come forward to you, within reason. We say "within reason" because there are limits in your world. You cannot, for example, create extreme destruction over and over again without causing a disruption in your containment field, or reality. When this disruption is heard, other beings come forward to limit you, to contain you. You are given leeway, as a child is given room inside a playpen. But you are not allowed out of that playpen until you are older and wiser and know how to care for yourself. Those are the limits that hold and protect you in your world.

Your world is a designed reality. You may say, "That cannot be. Everything around me is natural." And we say to you that it is surely natural in form, for in form it was created and all things exist in that realm. However, there are designs around your realm containing it, holding it in form, to give you the experience you desire. Once you step out of that design, you walk into realms of experience that are created for other beings, which are quite different from you.

If you tell yourself, "I live in this world, and it is a contraption designed for my experience," then your mind can expand. You can see your world as multidimensional. This allows you to be more flexible. You start seeing yourself as multidimensional, more able to experience new worlds as fluid beings who desire love and growth. This expands your world.

Question: But again, wouldn't Beach have already reincarnated? Did she just see a piece of him?

Your thinking is convoluted. You must expand how you see. If an individual desires to have an experience, the experience is brought forward. There are no limits to this beyond what we have expressed. There is a containment field, or reality, but within that field, you have the ability to create whatever you like. If you desire to see a loved one on the other side, he appears for you because that individual is a part of your realm, your universe. You could say that a portion of that individual remains in spirit no matter what the situation is around incarnations. But it is more complicated than that.

Let us say that a full self has many experiences at one time. These experiences unfold simultaneously. You may be an individual working on a railroad in one life, a sailor at sea in another life, and a worker on a spaceship in yet another life. All of these are in different times and locations, but they happen at once. The other side is formless, which is the point. It is from that place of formlessness that you create form for an experience. It is all for you to have an experience.

But you may say, "Oh, it is heaven. It is where people go when they die." And we say to you that the place you call heaven is also a construct. It is a fabrication of mind that allows you to have an experience. It is a fine experience, and you can create there all you like, but you can also see beyond it if that is your desire.

See beyond. See into the realms of the formless from which you create and knowingly create your world from there. See yourself as limitless and you shall have more fun. Then you can create ten images of the individual you desire to see and be satiated in that moment. You can experience love from your loved one and have it surround you. This can give you more joy than you know. If you expand your way of being, seeing, and experiencing and allow yourself to have more rather than fit your ideas into a limited universe, you expand your possibilities.

Chapter 16

Life Review

*When you review your life, you remember
to appreciate physical form rather
than criticize it.*

After you fully transition to the other side, you complete a life review. You evaluate your progress and ask questions of yourself. Did you accomplish what you planned to do in that life? Did you advance in your awareness? What would you like to do next?

This review process is a time of learning with love rather than a judgment day during which you receive criticisms from others. What were your defining moments and how could you have approached them differently? How can you make different choices and make your choices differently next time? How can you advance more quickly in your spiritual growth?

During her final years, Physsie reviewed her life extensively, determined more of what she liked and disliked, and made completions when she could. She determined that her first love was editing and helping us bring forward spiritual material, so she made the conscious commitment to help us with this book after she became acclimated on the other side. This meant that she would have to stick close to us in our physical reality for a while, and she was fine with that. Then, after she recuperated on the other side, she did her life review.

Question: Could you describe the life review process?

In this crystal city, you research who you are. You go through what is called a life review to see who you have been and understand your makeup as a conglomeration of energies. This is a self-discovery process. You review what you have done as a personality and build on that.

If your creations were faulty and you created negativity when you desired light, you review that. Where did your choices take you in a direction away from the light? What parts of your personality desired to do harm to you or others? What took you down a negative or dark path? What did you do that brought in more light? Once you see these things and understand the underlying learning experience you designed for your growth, you have an aha moment. This propels you forward in your creating.

If you say during your life review, "I wanted a big house, a fancy car, and a lot of money," then you are saying you desired things you did not create in that life. During your review, you ask yourself why you failed to create these things. If you created a small house, it could be that your primary goal was not a big house but to learn how to communicate in a close environment, under more challenging circumstances. If you had lived in a large house, you might have been too far removed from those you loved. Therefore, living in a small house helped you stay in the light and on-target with your life goals. Once you see this in your review and give thanks for experiencing your primary goal, you move on.

Question: If you do your best to gain awareness while you are alive, is there less of a life review on the other side?

Yes, for there is less time needed in rehabilitation and classrooms to review what you did, what you did not do, and the results. By choosing to review your situation during your lifetime, you enjoy the other side more fully and quickly when you arrive. You say to yourself, "I'm now in a place of creating without form. I can create more quickly and easily here. What a joy!"

When you review your life, you remember to appreciate physical form rather than criticize it. You notice how form gives you solid lessons. You are also aware of how frustration increases until you do what is required to receive the outcomes you desire. You notice how you are meant to experience joy and appreciation. Once you do this, you move along. When you are not experiencing joy, you know you have missed the mark.

As for Physsie, she did not have to review much because she reviewed her life before she died. She got tired of reviewing it, and that is what it takes. You have to get tired of it by answering all of your life's questions so you are complete. Physsie did this by writing and correcting her obituary, putting her family photos in albums, reading old letters, and talking to friends and family on the other side through Anne. She reviewed her life and felt complete with it.

Question: Can a life review be either formal or informal?

Yes. It can be less formal in nature because some individuals prefer that. The life review is done according to your desires and is designed to suit your needs. It is not set up to disturb you but to give you hope in moving ahead so you can see your options. You notice your unfulfilled desires and you choose what to do next.

Physsie went through a life review but did not see it as that. She felt she went to a short movie that was not a big deal. And when she speaks about it, she refers to everything she has learned about herself since she has been on the other side rather than speaking of an identifiable event or movie.

Physsie says, "I can't tell you exactly when I did a life review because everything seems to be more of an ongoing process. Whenever something comes to mind, it makes sense and is put into perspective for me. I now understand that I could have been more independent, more self-determining, and less able to be swayed by others."

Question: Can Physsie tell us more about her life review and the process in general?

Physsie says, "I did not want to do a formal review because I realized enough about myself before I passed. I have no plans of coming back into a physical body anytime soon so I don't need to recap everything again. I have found that when you desire to know something here, you know it. And if you do not desire to know it, then it doesn't come to mind. It is that simple.

"I know others have gone to formal movies about themselves during which they are shown who they are. They are generally less aware of themselves when they arrive, and when they see the movies, they are often shocked by some of the activities they were engaged in. They defend themselves and say why they did what they did. Some of them hold so tightly to a position that the situation is escalated. They are asked to participate more actively in their review so they can see themselves more clearly, and many don't want to do that.

"The ones who run the show are loving and kind, but some of the people who go through the process are zombie-like and energetically cannot really afford to do it. Some of them could use more rest and relaxation first. The process is set up to clean them out and prepare them for another life. It is designed to help them to regroup and see what they would like to do next, given what they have accomplished or not accomplished so far.

"Some break free of reincarnation by becoming aware and gaining wisdom over time. They pass their life reviews with flying colors and have the opportunity to stay on the other side and serve others as teachers, mentors, or guides. They are kind and assist others in fitting into the system, and some of these wiser individuals take helping positions in the library or schoolroom.

"In the school, people can learn anything they like, such as language, art, music, or gardening. They can pass their days gardening, as well. You simply desire any activity you like and it appears in front of you. You step into that image and you are there. This is how most people pass their time.

"It appears that most people are not completely conscious when they start engaging in activities. Even though they are moving around, their minds are somewhat on hold because they are still in the recuperation process. They are not completely functional, which is why they generally walk slowly unless they are engaged in an activity that requires speed. If they want to join the track and field team, then of course they speed up. In general, people engage in entertaining activities for a time even though the entertainment seems to me to be a bit artificial.

"Then they line up for their next lifetime. They stand in the queue, and when they get to the front, they ask, 'What are my options?' Their options appear in front of them. Maybe three images will show up, and they pick the image that feels right. Then they agree to enter that potential body, or body in the making, and they are back on the physical side of the wheel of life.

"They forget their life here in the afterlife and reenter the drama of physical humans. That drama has more of an adrenaline rush than is available to us on the other side. That is why it is so appealing. It is like a drug. Those feelings are like a rush through your energy system. On the other side, feelings are much more dummied down so you feel pleasant all the time. That is why heaven is considered to be a recuperation phase for getting back into life."

Question: Can you refuse a life review altogether?

Yes, you can do anything. However, the individuals who choose to leave the system before they become available for life review are those renegade personalities who prefer to work from nonphysical form and attach themselves to life forms without fully incarnating themselves. They simply hitchhike on other beings and have experiences without having to create bodies themselves. They come through the transition portal, the revolving door that takes you to the other side, and they quickly find their way back to the side of humanity and living form. That is their way of being, which they choose. There are many possibilities in this realm.

Question: Are you saying there are individuals who enter the physical realm without creating physical bodies?

Yes. After renegade personalities have been through the portal once as beings of form who have died, they have the option to return to the physical realm as beings without form. In the physical plane, they often attach to individuals with form. When those physical beings die and go to the other side, the attaching entities quickly scoot out of the afterlife because they have no interest in being retrained for accepting a lifetime with their own physical bodies. They do not desire to be specific by creating one individual body. They prefer to attach to an individual, a group of individuals, or a genetic line of individuals without having to produce a physical body for themselves. It is simply their desire to do so. You call these discarnates "possessing entities" or "attachments" when they attach themselves to another being.

As you can now see, you cannot assume that everyone follows the same process. They do not. There are a multitude of scenarios available to you.

Question: What did Physsie mainly learn from her life review?

The idea of finding her way home to herself was assigned to Physsie during her recent life review as a possibility for exploration in the afterlife and in her next incarnation. She took up this task. But when she chose to pursue this in the afterlife, she was not fully connected to her higher self and the wisdom that resides there. Her interpretation was that she needed to be independent of all others, including her higher self. This disconnected her somewhat more from the light.

We suggest that she stay connected to her higher self more fully in the afterlife so her experience there can become more fluid through space and time. Otherwise, she will attract those individuals who are darker in nature and desire to rule her world, for you see, when you travel without a clear connection to Source, you are easy prey to those who desire to maneuver

119

your body on either side. Therefore, a clear connection through your higher self to Source is desired at all times. This allows you a clean way to travel and access all the information you need.

PART THREE

Releasing Negativity

To release negativity you must see yourself as whole. You cannot see yourself as incomplete and expect completion to begin.

There are both light and dark unseen energies around you. Even though you may not be conscious of their presence, they can affect you dramatically in this life and in your transition to the next. Upon encountering negative unseen energy, you can feel good one minute and agitated and uncomfortable the next. You might assume that your emotions have gone haywire, but your emotions are actually picking up on the fact that you have just encountered foreign energy in your environment.

You can encounter negative unseen energy that comes from within you as your own negative beliefs or from outside of you as negative thought forms and negative energy beings. Beliefs are thoughts that you have had over and over again until they became solidified in your energy system. Thought forms are thoughts you and others have released into the ether like pollution that gathers with similar thoughts into a cloud of energy that floats through your reality. Energy beings are individual entities. These could be gremlins, which you can think of as elementals that enjoy wreaking havoc in your space. These could also be possessing entities, but those are rarer. Both can attach themselves to your energy system and cause difficulties.

By becoming aware of these energies, you empower yourself. You can choose to shift your thinking, alter your beliefs, and clean up your energy space. This allows you to feel better and bring more light into your world.

Negative Beliefs and Thought Forms

Desire creates form. Desire brings about all activities. If you desire to be at peace and transition in light, so be it. It is done.

B eliefs are habitual patterns of thinking. You have an experience and make a judgment about it in the form of a thought. And as you continue to think that thought, it becomes engrained in your energy system as a belief. These beliefs can be positive and supportive of your growth or negative and non-affirming of who you are as an independent, creative being. They can be adopted from your parents, culture, or religion. These beliefs bring about the creation of form in your world.

Thoughts are naturally emitted into the environment. As patterns of thinking continue, thoughts gain in strength and coagulate with similar repetitive thoughts. You could see them as clouds of energy, or thought forms, which float through the ether. You live in or walk through these at times.

When you have negative beliefs, or thought patterns, you unknowingly create situations that affirm those beliefs because like attracts like. You attract negative energies that encourage your negative thinking. Through watching the news and living in an unnatural world of gadgets and electronics, you can also weaken your system.

It is easy to lose touch with the earth and yourself when you rely so much on manmade devices. But you can counteract this negativity by becoming more focused on the light within you. As you become more aware of the energies around you and how they affect your world, you can choose to take action to repel or release negativity. Instead of fearing negativity, you can set boundaries and choose to think positive thoughts.

We asked the first of these questions while Physsie was still alive because she earnestly wanted to shift her thinking to be more positive as she drew closer to passing.

The Month Before Transitioning

Question: Over the years, Physsie has tried so hard to release negativity from her system. She saw intuitives, studied spirituality, called on her higher self, and meditated. In her essence, she is a loving, happy person. Why can't she release this negativity?

She did release some of her negative beliefs. You could say that she tried halfheartedly, though, because she truly desired for another to save her. We realize that you, as a people, are taught this idea of a savior from an early age, so it was not unusual for her to have these desires. She desired Beach to come to her rescue, even after he had crossed over to the other side. She kept looking outside of herself for love and saviors, even though you could say that she was independent in her thinking.

You see, ultimately, you must save yourself, and you all eventually learn this. You must choose the light within. When you do this, the angelic realm comes forward in joy to support you fully in love.

So bring in the light, claim your space, and love yourself more. Then angels surround you, for you have done your part by stating that you do not need another to save you. You are willing to stand tall and save yourself. When they see this, galleons of angels stand behind you. The fairy kingdom comes forward as well, and they are willing to battle and die for you as you move ahead in this energetic realm called Earth. This is truly kind on their part. It is an act of love and support, rather than an act of saving you.

Question: Yesterday, Physsie strongly asked the negativity to leave. What is her condition now?

Her desire is to be whole. Her attempts are halfway fulfilled because negativity still crowds into half of her being. This foils her attempts to achieve light. It is rarely heard of in this universe for someone to be so foiled and to choose to continue to move ahead. We suggest that you honor her for having done so much with so little light.

She must attempt to remove the remainder of darkness to continue. Her previous efforts are well noted, which is why we now say "attempt." She must desire more light to move ahead. It cannot be otherwise. You may also do a hands-on healing with her and request participation by her higher self in removing negativity and blocks from her system so more light may shine in. This activation process will assist her in moving ahead. It is appropriate now.

The negativity in her system is no longer tolerated by her. The prickles of energy that have held her back are becoming more obvious. This is the pain she is experiencing in her legs. These prickles of negativity have kept her from moving ahead. This negativity must be stopped through whatever means. She can continue in this lifetime if she desires to take that option.

As of now, she has more light in her system than she has had for many years. That has been achieved.

Question: How do you let go of negativity?

To release negativity you must see yourself as whole. You cannot see yourself as incomplete and expect completion to begin. This is a requirement. So if you see yourself as complete, as good as you are, then your abilities to move ahead are increased. Wholeness must be considered first. Then the energy of lack releases, for it is no longer necessary and it no longer has a place in your system.

As for Physsie, she has again chosen to transition and is in the process of doing so at this time. She is letting go of negativity in order to be whole. This requires the lessening of judgments and criticisms in her system. The hold that negativity had on her was intense. It required her to give up appreciating herself in favor of negativity and criticism of herself and others.

After Transitioning

Question: It has been a month since Physsie died. We held a space of light and love for her as she transitioned. How did she do in releasing negativity?

Before she left this reality, she said to herself, "I will be free!" This desire for freedom was acknowledged, and her system began recuperating before her spirit left her body completely. In other words, as she slept and desired wholeness, the activities of recuperation began. This process requires a peeling back of old systems. Permission was given by her higher self to begin the process while she was living in this reality.

You may wonder how that can be done, and we say to you, desire creates form. Desire brings about all activities. If you desire to be at peace and transition in light, so be it. It is done. You do not need to be in pain for your transition. Your desire, when it is pure, creates your reality. Of course, when you desire conflicting things at once, you get convoluted results.

Chapter 18

Gremlin Energy

As you bring light into darkness, it eliminates darkness, and that is the realm of gremlins.

As you have adventures on Earth, you can naively make agreements or contracts with people that seem fine at the time but turn out to not be acting in your best interests. You can make similar agreements with energies that are unseen. As you grow and become stronger within yourself, you can realize that these agreements no longer serve you. But it is often hard to change old agreements because they have become familiar patterns in your energy system.

You could call these negative unseen beings gremlins. Gremlins could be thought of as mischievous elementals that enjoy causing problems. They enter your space when you need help in some way. You call out in desperation and innocently agree to accept their assistance. For example, if you were drowning, you would grab the arm of anyone who said he would save you. You might invite him to your home for a meal to thank him. And if he said he needed a place to stay for a few nights, you would most likely invite him to stay, given he has just saved your life. Over time, this houseguest could take up residence in your home and eventually wreak havoc in your life.

You could say that gremlins work for the dark side, even though all darkness is ultimately in service to the light. They are like little soldiers who live and reproduce in less light.

Beyond gremlins, there are other negative unseen beings called possessing entities that have chosen to decrease the light in their world. They have chosen to reject love in favor of greed and control, though even they may not be aware that they have repeatedly made the choice to do so. They are no different from people who have made similar choices, but they are operating without a physical body because they have chosen to attach to another's energy system rather than create a body for themselves. We will only discuss them briefly because they are less frequently experienced in our world than gremlins.

Gremlins became apparent in Physsie's energy field as she got closer to passing. They wanted to stay in control. As Physsie's desire to transition into the light increased, the gremlins became more agitated. But with the help of her higher self, loving unseen beings, and our determination, these gremlins moved on. This allowed Physsie to bring in more light during her transition.

Question: Could you describe a gremlin?

A gremlin is simply an energy pattern that desires destruction in your world. It takes actions to do so by entering the space of those who emit light and desire light. It makes its job to snuff out that light because it desires an increase in darkness rather than light. As soon as happiness begins growing in an individual's space, the gremlin goes after the light of happiness to pat it down and put it out. It is like a game in which the light is like a ball that the gremlin goes after. If you desire to have more joy, self-acceptance, and love, you must deter the gremlins by camouflaging or hiding your light and making yourself uninteresting to them. To do this, you must maintain healthy boundaries and an energy system that is formidable.

If you go to Disneyland, you will see a wall around the theme park. You will pay for a ticket to gain admission. We suggest that you create the same setup for admission to your energy system. Create a wall around you that defines your area and allow in only those individuals to whom you have given a ticket after they have read and duly accepted your policies. Your policies state that this place—your energy system—is for having fun and creating joy, and anyone who breaks your rules is removed easily and swiftly.

You, the owner of your theme park, have the right to set rules and manage your park any way you see fit. By recognizing this, you set boundaries and state to the universe that you mean business. No gremlins will apply for admission because they know better than to go to the gate to buy a ticket when they cannot sign your policy form. Their desire is to lessen your light, decrease the joy in your system, and eliminate the pure fun you are having so they can drop your energy flow and dim your light. With increased laughter and joy, the flow of your energy increases, sparks of light are ignited, and you become brighter.

Remember, gremlins desire to influence you and put out the campfire within you because it is enjoyable to them. When you say, "Gremlins stop doing that!" you are telling them that they can no longer have fun at your expense. Eventually, based on their own desires, they will seek enjoyment through your pain. Therefore, it is better to recognize the differences in desires and disengage from them in the beginning so everyone can be happy. Eventually, everyone learns about boundaries and the realms of creating, so you can let the gremlins go from your space so they can attach to those people who still need to learn through pain.

If you appreciate a gremlin for what it truly is—an aspect of darkness that is ultimately in service to the light—it will soften and its light will increase slightly through your love. However, we recommend that you do this infrequently, for if you keep at it, gremlins will come after you with fervor, desiring to destroy you. In their minds, you are destroying them.

Remember, as you bring light into darkness, it eliminates darkness, and that is the realm of gremlins. But if you love briefly and then leave them alone, you have introduced light into their systems without judgment or interference. This is you simply loving and appreciating all things in your universe. Then quickly take your attention and place it back upon yourself.

Question: How does Lewis Bostwick describe gremlins? What do they look like?

They are energy beings who interfere with your life. Their intention is to do harm. You have seen personality shifts in those around you. This often occurs after a gremlin has jumped into someone's energy space and has influenced the person's behavior. This is a level down from possessing entities. Possession involves a being who intends evil and has more clout and more ability to carry it through. Gremlins, on the other hand, are like little elemental soldiers who are not of your realm but interfere with it.

You could say that gremlins have been known to cause the breakdown in computers and mechanical devices. They find a dark alleyway to travel through and consider that to be their world. They are like crazed rodents who chew up wires and destroy the place. They can look like short, rectangular beings, usually six inches to a foot tall, with no necks and no waistline.

Question: How did Physsie communicate with them to invite them in?

Well, they were there just as energies of light were there. She could have called upon fairies, but she did not. She said, "I am lonely," so the fairies waited for her to be happy because they want to be happy. But the gremlins said, "Oh, we play in the dark realm of unhappiness so we can come play with you." And that's what happened. It was a natural match because negativity is all around.

Question: Are gremlins thought forms?

No, not exactly. They are energy systems that have been designed to wreak havoc in your world. They are like miniature mechanical devices. Their intention is to cause harm, for that brings them joy. They do this by lying to you and telling you they can make you feel better when you are lonely and when you want help. Those are their two main inroads.

When you say, "I cannot do it myself. I need help in maneuvering this situation," or when you say, "I am so lonely, please make me feel better," you can attract greater negative energies once the gremlins are in because your energy system is weakened and an entryway has been created. You could say that gremlins work for the negative energies that inhabit your world. They are most similar to elementals.

Question: Why did Physsie let the gremlins take over her life?

She simply allowed them to do so. It is like a fungus that grows if it goes untreated. They desired to take over her space as a fungus would, and they did because Physsie did not defend her space in the beginning. Gremlins are in your world to show you where the weaknesses are in your boundary system. You must set boundaries and care for yourself. They assist you in learning to care for yourself.

Question: Why are gremlins able to get into your space?

When you experience drama or negativity, you experience the pain of loss. As a result, you often vacate your system, giving gremlins the space to come in. For example, Physsie experienced shock, emotional pain, and loneliness when her first husband, Beach, died. When she heard her second husband was having affairs, she experienced betrayal and separation. When her beloved father died, she once again experienced emptiness, loneliness, and separation. These are all negative reactions that allow negativity to get into your space.

You could say you go dark for a time and, therefore, can become darker. People do not realize that when they enter pain, their light diminishes. This attracts other negativity. Depression can begin with a thought of sadness that is multiplied when a gremlin enters the system.

Question: Is having gremlins in your space similar to being possessed?

True, to some degree. When you ask for assistance and it is given through any beings of less light, they often have the desire to run your world. They have desires or agendas of their own. And since you requested their assistance, you gave them permission to enter your energy system. It does you no good to say, "Oh, this gremlin moved in. Dreadful gremlin. I hate this gremlin." Instead, you must say, "I invited in this gremlin for some reason. What was I thinking? I was not thinking clearly at that time. I forgive myself. Now I will retract that invitation by stating that I choose to bring in only light and love as guidance at this time. I also request that the hiring of this guidance go through the scrutiny of my higher self to ensure that I bring in only vibrations that are higher and wiser than me in this area of consideration. I want energy that brings me up instead of pulling me down."

Question: *How do gremlins handle being around the light?*

They handle it by snuffing it out. You see you are not yet completely light. You have many areas within you that are darkness. These are areas that lack self-approval and self-love. A gremlin can maneuver through your energy system, through those dark alleyways, and when it sees light coming from a place, such as underneath a doorway, it can block the light by putting something like a blanket there. As long as the gremlin travels in areas that are mainly dark, it is fine and can exist there for eons. That is why it is best to eliminate the possibility of gremlins entering your system by stating that only light beings may apply for entry at your front gate.

Question: *Why do so many people still have gremlins in their space even though they have done their best to get rid of them?*

Gremlins travel in darkness. There is much darkness around you and within you no matter what you do or who you are. There are areas within you that are unclean or impure due to a lack of self-love. Even the brightest of you will, most likely, have an area that is lacking light. You may call this darkness your shadow or your shadow self.

As long as you are incarnating, you have some darkness within you. You are born into the physical plane in order to discover yourself and uncover those areas that have less light.

In this way, you may heal yourself and bring yourself back to wholeness through love. Once you introduce love into an area in your system, the light returns.

Question: Does grounding to the earth and connecting to the light of Source help you clear your space of gremlins?

Yes. Through grounding into this reality that you call life, you become more fully present and see more clearly. It is similar to gathering your energy on the other side, only you do this before your so-called death. This is highly suggested, for when you see more clearly, you request more light because you realize that you want to see even more. Experiencing some enlightenment often brings about the desire for more enlightenment, of having more light in your being. You want to connect to Source, be more creative, and enjoy your life more fully. When you focus on the light, you gain much in awareness and the snowball starts rolling down the hill, gaining in speed and magnitude.

Question: If gremlins are beings, how do they evolve?

You may see gremlins as those particles of light that have become dim over time. They have forgotten they are God. They believe they must attach to another to be whole. This is incorrect. Once they remember that they are God in their realm, they will stand tall, feel good about themselves, and recall that they have the ability to create as light beings.

They can advance up the stream of energy and look forward to creating bodies of their own. They will no longer need to attach to others to feel themselves as whole. When this occurs, the energies you call gremlins will retire. They will no longer be an experience in your world.

As you love yourself more as an individual being with a body, you will have no need for an attachment, such as a gremlin, to bring you down. You do not need them to remind you that you are a whole through your experience of lack of wholeness, misery, and victimhood. When you love yourself more and have no need for attachments, gremlins find themselves out of a job and experience self-reflection. They have no purpose as gremlins anymore. They must redefine themselves, otherwise they have no need for existence. That is an awakening in their world.

This is another level of returning to Source. It is the elimination of the lower levels of existence, which are the experiences that lack light. This is where you, as a people, are headed. You are headed to experience yourselves with more love and more light.

Chapter 19

Grappling with Gremlins

*Each time you see negativity coming
towards you, choose the light.*

A month before Physsie crossed over, she had a dream about gremlins that really scared her. They were short stumpy beings with no necks, dressed in tattered pieces of cloth. They flew around her room, some of them in charge and some taking orders, as soldiers would. She felt they were doing their jobs, so she couldn't fault them for that. She had seen these gremlins seven years earlier in the hospital when she almost died. At that time, they were of all shapes and sizes, and they came at her directly. She called them oogly-googlies.

That month before she passed, Physsie wanted to know about these flying beings. She asked All That Is questions about how to remove them from her space. Based on these channeled conversations, she made her decision to remove them.

One week before she passed, these gremlins finally left her space through her intense desire to clear out her negativity, coupled with her desire to bring in her higher self, angels, guides, and us to hold her in love as she brought in more light. We finally saw the sweetness and loving kindness we recognized but had not seen in years. The real Physsie had made it through. She was now filled with love and not negativity. We wept in gratitude because it had been such a long road.

Then we asked more questions about these gremlins six months after she died.

A Month Before Transitioning

Question: Why was Physsie able to see these gremlins flying round her bedroom when we were out of the house?

These were energies dwelling in Physsie's space that she expelled and placed in front of her so she could see them more clearly. They were causing havoc in her system, and the light, the positive energy in her system, was no longer willing to accommodate this negativity. To move into the light more fully, which is her desire, she must release negativity from her system.

These entities do not want her to grow, so they were increasing her pain level in order for her to experience more physical discomfort, disease, and the inability to be herself. When you were out of the house, she cried out, "No, I will have no more of this pain!" Then she saw how her world had been taken over by these energies. This vision created more choice. Her ability to see them allowed her to decide if she desired to keep them or completely eliminate them from her system.

They would come in more strongly when you two were out of the house because their opportunity to control her was greater then. When you three held the light together, they were suppressed and went into hiding because they knew better than to come out. But when you left the house, they felt they could own the place. That was when Physsie said, "No!" and then saw them. Their ownership of her is no longer appropriate.

Question: Physsie did not like seeing them. She asks, "Why is this happening to me now? I have been down this road before with these oogly-googlies and I don't want to go there again."

It is happening again because the choice you have to make is bigger now. You are allowed options, so you are being shown the future and what it would be like to go to the dark side to help you determine whether or not you want that experience. Going to the dark side means that you would attempt to live in the space of negativity for a long time. Would you like that? That is what it looks like to think negative thoughts and allow negativity to take over.

You are at a decision point where you can choose what you would like to do with more clarity. Seeing the gremlins in your room makes it clearer, does it not? Your vision of them is simply making things obvious for you. You could say that you have given yourself the gift of clarity. When you have truly chosen to let go of negativity, these negative energies will be gone and your spine will be aligned with light. That will allow you to move freely with love. We see that as your goal.

So choose the light. That is all that is required. Each time you see negativity coming towards you, choose the light. It is simpler than you think. But it may take two to three weeks to complete this process, so be patient with yourself in the meanwhile. That is a kindness you must give to yourself with love.

Question: How can Physsie make the clear decision to remove them? Can you help us with this?

The decision has been made. She claimed her space as of a few minutes ago. When she said to herself, "I will have nothing to do with this!" they left her space. Now it is time for things to settle in.

Question: Physsie responds, "They didn't like that, did they! But now what do I do?"

If you choose to continue with that fervor—that decision, that commitment—they will not return. By the laws of the universe, they cannot return. We would say, "Keep it up!"

Question: So is Physsie claiming the purity of light and love from Source?

She is claiming her space as her dominion. She is choosing to populate the area around her with light, angelic beings, fairies, and animals that are kind and good. They will protect her from other energies that attempt to take over her being because she has requested this and has hired them to do so.

Question: Physsie responds, "Will they always be knocking at my door?"

Once you claim your space and love yourself more thoroughly, they will give up. But it may take a few weeks to do this. We acknowledge that it has been a challenge to wait so long, but that it is a definitive time frame. If it is worth weeks to you in an eternity of light, we suggest that you choose patience and the light.

Six Months After Transitioning

Question: It has been six months since Physsie died. Could you tell us more about the gremlins she saw flying around her room that month before she died?

She was seeing who she was. She had become negative by allowing negativity in. Becoming aware that she had been overcome by gnats of negativity helped her recognize she did not want that anymore. Seeing those hobo beings float around her room made her clearly aware of her situation, even though they had been there all along.

In the beginning, she was not as aware that they had taken over her world. When she saw them floating around her in the room, she could choose more easily to say no to having them rule her. The awareness of her situation and making the clear choice to not want them made them leave. She was bigger than they were, and she had simply forgotten that.

You may say, "Yes, she desired them into her space in the first place. But why couldn't she kick them out before?" And we say to you that she could not kick them out because she still desired to have them. After a time, she felt she would be lonely without them.

In the last days of her life, Physsie wholeheartedly decided that she would not put up with them, no matter what the alternative was. She made a clear choice to have them leave her space. Before that, she waffled. When you waffle, the negativity remains. It does not leave when it sees it has an opening, even if it is a small one. But when you say, "No more. I'm done with this!" and put them on the other side of the door and lock it, they have no option but to stay out.

Question: Did the gremlins in Physsie's space accentuate her dementia?

Yes. They made her angry and miserable and caused her great agitation. As she desired to see more clearly, they took over and grabbed her mind. They told her she was not enough, incomplete, and unsatisfied. As she desired to grow and love herself more, they created hell in her realm. These energies of darkness took over, for she had left her body unprotected in her dreams, and they had the opportunity to return and mess with her. You could say that she had vacated her world somewhat.

These energy beings of less light come in when you are unsure of yourself. Lack of assuredness creates an opportunity or opening for other energies. They generally take this opportunity to take over your world. It is like termites moving in.

This is how the world is constructed. When you leave a space or lay less claim to it, others choose to take over. It is similar to laying a claim to a piece of land. If you later vacate it, another will say, "Oh, look! Here is a free piece of property. I think I shall claim it as my own." And the vagrant takes over your space. When you return and say, "Wait a minute, this was my land. Get out of here!" the vagrant may say, "I don't think so. I claimed it as my own." Then an argument ensues that can last a long time.

This is why Physsie remained so detached in the end. She was fighting these gremlins as best she could on an unconscious level, and she had forgotten her way home. This was distracting for her. She desired love and light and could not find it until the very end when she made her declaration and you held the space for her to be herself. This is when her spirit returned to occupy her body more fully in the form of her higher self and she said, "Oh, good. I have a moment of rest now. I have a moment to regroup before I go to the other side more fully."

This was a treat for her. She wanted to be more present with you before that, but circumstances did not allow it. She had lost control of her property and could not regain it. She gave up, and in letting go of her resistance, the vision of her situation was able to come through. By letting go of the fight, she was able to be herself once again. Her energy was returned and she was able to complete with you before passing.

Loneliness and Lack Attract Gremlins

The game cannot be played if you believe yourself to be whole. Therefore, rise above it. Laugh at the negativity and the positivity that fights it, for the fight brings you down. Rise above it to that place of wholeness and self-appreciation.

When you feel lonely, you find ways to fill the hole inside you. You look for friends, activities, and addictions to fill the gaps when you are alone. Of course, you are not alone at all because you are connected to your higher self, your guides, seen and unseen friends, and Source. But when you are lonely, you have already forgotten that you are whole and that only you can truly fill the hole from the inside.

Physsie felt desperately alone after the shock of her fist husband's death when she was thirty. When she was around eighty, many close friends died, a romantic relationship ended, and she moved away from her longtime home. In an attempt to fill the emptiness from the outside, she watched television and unconsciously made agreements that allowed unseen energies to move into her energy system. These beings were not of pure light because she forgot to specify that she wanted only beings of pure light. These gremlins took over more as the years progressed, as can be typical when one is lonely.

Question: When did Physsie's loneliness take over?

Loneliness became prevalent in her system around eleven years ago after she moved from her home in Missouri to be near you. Before she moved, she was active socially and romantically, but soon after she moved, she saw that her potential for relationship was no longer a possibility. She desired love but did not know when it would come again. She did not miss her old home as much as she missed her love life. She felt empty and dark inside and did not want to be alone. Before this, she had hope and thought something would eventually change. After this, when her friends started dying in numbers, she felt more and more alone.

Question: Did Physsie regret moving to Colorado?

Physsie says, "No, not at all!" She tremendously appreciates moving to Colorado to be with you. She would have had this loneliness whether or not she moved. Her loneliness was not from her changing locations but from her evaluation of her future.

Question: Did Physsie stay up all night watching TV so she could guard against these gremlins?

She says she stayed up to feel better. She wanted to feel alive again. These dark shadows filled her bedroom at night, and she sensed she had no space for herself. She watched TV in an attempt to ignore the feeling of frustration about their having taken over

146

her world. She hoped to feel better when she went to sleep because they told her they would take care of her loneliness, and truly, they did fill her room. But she just felt crowded out of her own space. She felt she couldn't breathe, so it was worse. That is why she stayed up. She was afraid that they would take over even more if she went to sleep completely, so she was continuously on guard.

Looking at it now, she says that towards the end, she was so obsessed with keeping them out of her space that it was like fighting off a swarm of gnats. She was continuously agitated and had no time to appreciate what was around her. She was only concerned with the gnats. No matter how loving you were towards her, she could not feel it because she was focused on the gnats.

Question: What can you do before you go to bed to avoid this situation? How do you get away from these gremlins?

You can claim your space and say, "I love me. I love my physical body. I love every inch of it, and I claim it now." Claim your space for yourself. Negative energies reside in darker realms, for they are incomplete and lack light.

The game cannot be played if you believe yourself to be whole. Therefore, rise above it. Laugh at the negativity and the positivity that fights it, for the fight brings you down. Rise above it to that place of wholeness and self-appreciation. Ask that your higher self participate more fully. That will increase the vibration of love.

Physsie's higher self felt shunned and put on the shelf because she cherished another so fully—her first husband who had died. She cherished him more than she cherished her higher self. That needed to switch from another being her God to her being in charge of her world. The focus needed to move from an outward other to an inward higher self.

The issue is bigger than the idea that you must increase your vibration. The decision must be made to believe in yourself and not rely on another. It is a matter of choosing. You can choose by saying the words, "I love me." The more you say this, the higher your vibration will become. This creates a pattern of indwelling for you.

This negative pattern of energies is widespread on Earth. Discomfort can increase as the negativity resists the light and you move them out. You must be willing to move through it, repeat your desires, and believe in yourself as whole. Soothing music can assist you in this.

Question: Physsie, now that you have been on the other side a while and have a different perspective, could you explain your loneliness and the gremlins moving in?

Physsie says, "I wanted companionship. I wanted someone to be there with me in the late hours of the night. I called in the gremlins without knowing what I was doing. I can explain this better now that I have a bigger perspective.

"The last eleven years of my life were a challenge. I watched TV for a long time because I felt that might fill the void. I thought that watching politics would make me feel that I was still a part of a team. But that feeling didn't last, and I still felt alone at night.

"The unseen energies—the gremlins—were able to tempt me when I first moved to Colorado by saying, 'Do you want a friend? We will be your friends.' And I wanted to believe them. When I saw the love in relationships around me, I wanted that. In the wee hours of the night, I could not bear seeing myself living the rest of my life alone, so I let them in at some unconscious level.

"Soon I found that these gremlins had their own agendas at heart. They were not being kind, even though they said they were there for me. I should have looked more closely at them before I let them in because they were up to no good. It's my own fault for not having caught that.

"At first, I stood up to them and told them I knew they could not make me feel better because I had figured that out. I told them I had decided that I was quite satisfied with my life even though I had fewer friends. It was just in those wee hours of the night when I missed another's touch that they got me. They said, 'We can cure your loneliness by being with you all night,' and I really wanted to believe them.

"In the beginning, they came and went, so their group alternated in size from one to sometimes two or three. Then they called in their friends. Pretty soon it wasn't just a couple of them but a party of five. At night they would sit in five chairs around my bed and tell me they could make me feel better. In the morning when I told them I was awake, so they could leave, they would say, 'We'd really like to stay in the daytime as well.'

"So I would be accommodating and say, 'Fine. I'll get about my day and you can get about yours.' But I soon began to feel crowded and agitated. I would go to the bathroom to brush my teeth and they would be there with me. I no longer had any privacy because they were always there. In looking back, I can now see what caused me to be so agitated that last five or six years.

"In the end, it was even worse because I didn't know who I was anymore. I felt lonely even though they were ever present because they were not loving. I kept looking for solace but couldn't find it. That is why I kept drinking root beer. I kept telling myself that I would feel better soon, that I had to because this could not continue.

"It wasn't until the very end that I realized I was the one in charge. I had the ability to live or die! I did not have to put up with this anymore. Knowing that I could make my own decisions and get away from those beings made me feel better and more empowered. They said they were of the light, but they were not. They were darker than even they knew, and I finally see that.

"I would tell anyone who is looking for love to feel better to first consider themself. Do not think you need someone else to fill you because this is what can happen when you are lonely and want someone to be there for you. These shadowy beings can fill your space, and then there is no space left for you. It does not feel good. It simply fills you. This has been a hard road for me, and I want to warn you so you can avoid this trap. I'm not saying that I have all the answers, but I do know that I wouldn't repeat this experience."

Question: Physsie, did living with us (Anne and Greg) agitate the gremlins in your space?

Physsie says, "Yes. They didn't like you because you said you didn't want any negativity in your home when I moved in with you three years ago. They said you were unintelligent and not a part of their world. They considered you two to be poor hosts because they were used to getting their way when I lived alone. And the more they took over my space, the more they convinced me that you were intruding on their space. They thought you were claiming a part of the world that should be theirs. Therefore, you were the bad guys. You were the ones who pushed them out and didn't let them stay and play everywhere in the house. They just wanted to sit on your living room floor and play games, and you kept showing them the door. They said that was rude, and they had nothing but disdain for you.

"There were so many of them towards the end—maybe seven to ten most of the time—that I had only a small space to breathe. They filled my room because you wouldn't let them be in the rest of the house. The part of me that was truly me, the real Physsie, couldn't shine until that very last week when I said, 'Enough is enough,' and kicked them out. I felt so good about that. Many people think you need religion or a father or mother to tell you what to do, but that isn't true. You just have to tell yourself what you want and not get taken over by bullies who tell you they are your friends."

Question: Physsie, if you had connected more to your higher self, would that have taken care of the issues of loneliness and gremlins?

"Yes, that would have been a good idea. My higher self could have told me what I wanted to know. I forgot that. Before, when I was desperate, I thought I had to do it all my little self, and that got me into trouble with the gremlins. It was my disappointment and feelings of loneliness that brought on that negativity in the first place. I'll be more careful and aware of the light now. My higher self and guides are telling me that I need more time recuperating and revitalizing myself through Source. I will do that."

151

PART FOUR

Guidance and Support

Your positive actions increase the vibration in your field and your energy system becomes filled with sparks of light and love for yourself that attract more light and love around you.

There is tremendous support from unseen beings, whether you notice it or not. Your higher self is always available to you. Spirit guides come in when you make agreements with them, and angels, archangels, and guardian angels stand by you to support you with love when you need it.

Given you have free will, you can request, accept, or reject unseen assistance. And the assistance available to you ranges from excellent to disappointing. You can grow and become brighter through your experiences with this guidance or you can become dimmer by following advice that was either inappropriate for you or that you have misinterpreted. It is always up to you to make good choices and be the captain of your destiny, even when you request and receive support.

If your tube for receiving intuition is cloudy, then the information you receive from guidance may be limited or faulty. To remedy this, you can cleanse yourself through practicing intuition exercises.

Chapter 21

Your Higher Self

*When you choose to communicate
more with Source through your higher
self and full self, you become lighter
and your experiences in form can
be synchronous and in flow.*

The higher self, which is not in the physical realm, is the wiser part of you. It helps you stay on your path without interfering with your choices. You can communicate with it to receive advice and direction. It is always available to help because it is a part of you, and it truly desires for you to grow and merge with it. You could see your higher self as the wiser future you, your ultimate guide.

By becoming more aware of your higher self connection, your communication with it can be easier and more natural. Through this more aware connection, you can create from a space of greater wisdom and higher perspective. You can live your life more fully and with greater enjoyment when you and your higher self communicate well. This same desire for connection may continue in the afterlife.

Question: *What is the higher self and how is it related to the body?*

The energy you call your higher self is evidenced in your world through wisdom. It is your access to Source. You can see it as a beam of light coming into you as ideas when you are at your most creative. This is your true self. It is you at your best. This part of you is available to you at all times when requested, but you must request its presence.

When you, as a personality, incarnate into a physical body of your choosing, you leave behind a part of you in a higher vibration. This is your higher self. You could say that it remains in spirit so you can maintain perspective in your world of form. This gives you a fighting chance in the world you call "reality." Your higher self is there for you when you mess up and look for better answers. It is your best friend because it is your access to higher wisdom, your connection to Source. It has your highest good at heart and has nothing else to do but be there for you. It is you from a higher perspective.

When you incarnate, you take a part of yourself, a droplet of who you are, and drop it into the physical body you created for yourself. When you do this, your physical body comes to life. When it is in the womb of your mother, it is sparked by you and fed by the mother. This is the process of one physical form giving birth to a replication of itself in a newly created form.

When birth occurs, the spark that is you takes charge of the new physical form and is responsible for it. It is as if you are on a horse and the reins are handed to you. You must steer the horse, which is your new body and life. When this happens, you are mostly connected to your higher wisdom, for you have just left the other side.

Question: Could you describe the relationship between the higher self and Source?

The system you consider to be you, which you identify by your name, is quite complicated. By that, we mean you are a world within a world within a world. You are more than you experience yourself to be.

You have your lower self, which includes your physical body and is overseen by your higher self. Your higher self is held within the reality of your spirit, or full self. Your full self is an emanation of being from Source.

There are many emanations that come from Source. It is like many strings hanging down with many knots in them. Your being is one of these strings with knots. Each knot on your string represents an experience of fullness or wholeness unto itself. As the knots drop down, there is another experience and another and another. Each knot is its own experience, yet it is connected through the string to other knots and ultimately connected back to source.

You can see the knots as parts of your being. You are every knot, but your current experience of yourself is your most physical knot at the end of the string. This is the lowest or densest knot. It is your focus in this lifetime. It is both your form and your creation.

When you appreciate your form and see yourself as more than form, you move up a knot and access the wisdom of your higher self. This higher self is there for you in spirit to support you in this and all your lifetimes. By acknowledging your spirit, you appreciate that which is beyond your physical body. You experience yourself as more of who you are.

Moving up the string further, you find your full self, which had the thought to create you as form in this world through your personality. You could say that your personality, which develops over lifetimes of experiences, desires to have experiences. It has free will and desires to create.

This personality self can choose to communicate with its higher self once it is in form. When it chooses not to communicate, it is like a rogue being and can have experiences that become darker and darker. This is the experience of self-sabotage, for you have allowed in darker energies to rule your world.

On the other hand, when you choose to communicate more with Source through your higher self and full self, you become lighter and your experiences in form can be synchronous and in flow. When you are more connected to Source, things move more easily and you receive those things you desire more simply.

There are fewer learnings experienced as difficulties when you are more connected to Source. Your answers flow smoothly because your questions are well received. In other words, your connection or tube to Source through your higher self is cleaner, so your questions and requests go to Source more easily and the answers and fulfillments of your desires come back to you more simply and quickly. When your tube to Source is cloudy and clogged with less light flowing through it, the answers you receive can be limited and your experiences can be challenges, more often than not.

Question: This is hard to understand. Could you again describe the relationship of the personality to the higher self, the full self, and Source?

As for the energy of your being and how it could be described, let us say that you have your physical form, which includes your personality. Your personality, or lower self, can be described as that part of you that includes the challenges you have had throughout your experiences. Your experience could be defined as lifetimes or nonlinear simultaneous experiences.

These experiences act as feedback that keeps coming back to you until you receive your specific learnings. You, as your higher self, deemed these learnings to be important for you to move through in order to return to the light of Source, the subtler emanation of spirit.

Above your personality on the string, you can see your higher self. The higher self could be seen as an energy system, not in form, that hovers above the physical form and is available to it. The personality in form must choose to stay in contact with the higher self. The personality, which you could see as the child, must choose to receive wisdom from the higher self, or parent. Otherwise, the higher self sits and waits for the lower self, which is the personality self, to ask for its wisdom. It is like a good parent who lets her child have experiences but is there for that child upon request.

Above the higher self on that string is your full self. Within the full self are all the experiences of your being. All things are connected and encompassed within the full self. Up the string from the full self is Source. This gives you a general description of the relationship even though it is actually more complex.

Question: Could you explain more about the relationship of the full self to Source?

Basically, Source ejects a string of light with a spark of light as a knot at the end of it. That spark finds a place in the fabric of love where it wants to be, and when the time is right, it ignites itself as your full self. The full self is the one who initially wanted to have an experience of being. It births your higher self and personality.

Above the full self is Source, or the ultimate being of light that initially birthed the spark. You could describe the light as the masculine aspect because you are birthed out of the light, which went out and found its home in the fabric of love. Love could then be described as the receiving, or feminine, aspect. You could say that Source is that light, or central sun, or grand creator, around which is the fabric of love, the deep dark space that holds within it the light.

Question: When we were first ejected as sparks of light, which also can be seen as a string of knots, was our personality and higher self one or did they start out as separate?

It depends how far back you go. In the beginning, you were a spark of light. That nucleus became you. You went out and had experiences, and as you did so, you forgot you were God, creator in your realm. The farther away you moved from Source, the dimmer you became. As this occurred, you forgot you were God and forgot that you had everything within you. When you forgot, you broke away from your wisdom. You said to yourself, "I don't need that connection. I know what I want to do. I am independent." So you dropped away and became dimmer. From the experience of being whole, you gave birth to a new idea, the idea that you were not whole. The universe is set up to allow for that.

You said to yourself, "I do not need the light. I am smart and clever. I shall make it on my own." And because you have free will and choice, you were allowed to continue thinking you were God in disconnection from wholeness. But as you return to Source, as your wisdom increases, you desire more and more to be whole. And to be whole you must remember you are God, creator in your realm, a being of light connected to Source and the fabric of love.

In your disconnection, you may say to yourself, "Oh, I know I am a creator in my realm." And we say to you, surely, you are. But you have forgotten much of your light. You have forgotten much of your connection to Source. When you remember that and desire to go home, you desire to connect more fully with your higher wisdom. Your higher self is simply the wisdom that is one step ahead of you.

As you start connecting more to the whole of who you are, your lower self (less wise self, more dense self, ego, personality self) desires to connect more with your higher self, and that integrates your personality. When you do this, you have access to Source and not just the artificial idea of Source from your personal ego. Your ego developed an idea of itself that was somewhat faulty. It thought it was God, but it was not in full form because God in full form is bright light.

Question: *Is it a good goal, then, to integrate the personality with the higher self?*

True, very much so, for that is you returning home to wholeness. In the beginning, simply recognizing that you have a higher self that has access to Source wisdom is of huge benefit. You must truly conceive of that and not believe that another is your god. Many feel the government should tell you what to do, or the church should give you guidance, but instead, you must look to yourself.

In the beginning, access to Source through your higher self may seem quite faulty. It is rather like pipes that have become rusty over time. It is difficult for any information to pass through them. Though it is an ordeal, a personal decision to clean out the pipes is required for you to return to Source. It requires much attention and love, which is why many individuals choose not to do it. They would rather turn on their electronics and let another entertain them and tell them what to do.

As you continue to choose activities with less light, you move downward in your vibration and become dimmer. This momentum makes it difficult to reverse the downward spiral. It is like being flushed down a toilet. It is a challenge to crawl out. But once you choose to crawl up and out and welcome the light into your being, you are supported. You are assisted through your higher self, guides, angels, and unseen beings of light.

Question: Does this time in our history help us return to the light and our higher selves?

True, very much so. The particles of light that are entering your universe at this time are meant to awaken you. It is as if an airplane has dropped confetti in your world—it cannot be ignored because it is landing on you. Some individuals will say, "Get this confetti off of me. It irritates me!" And they will choose to eliminate the light particles from their world because they see them as irritants. These are the individuals who desire less light, and that is their prerogative. However, if you desire to grow and receive more light, you appreciate the light particles that stimulate your system. You give thanks for your growth because you know you are expanding in love.

Chapter 22

Spirit Guides

If you want true guidance, we suggest that you communicate more fully with your higher self, which is that part of you that is wise and connected to Source.

Spirit guides are available to assist you during your time on Earth. They can be with you for a short time or your whole life, depending on your needs. They can even accompany you across several lifetimes. You can have many or a few of them, and they can come with specific abilities or a wide range of information. Guides can also flow through genetic lines.

Guides may be helpful or not so helpful, and they can come with a little or a lot of awareness. You can consciously or unconsciously request them to assist you. It is important to remember that you are meant to be the one in charge. That they are guides does not mean they know what is best for you. The goal is to know that these beings are present in your reality, let go of the ones that no longer serve you, and appreciate the help you receive from those who reside in the purest light and help you become more enlightened.

Your ancestors can be your guides as well. Like spirit guides, they can be helpful or not so helpful, and their beliefs and programming can flow to you through your genetic lines. Through your intention, you can replace inherited beliefs with thought patterns that are right for you at this time. You can heal your genetic line and lifetimes for yourself.

Question: What is a spirit guide?

That is an individual who comes forward as a volunteer to assist you in making decisions in your life. If you have questions and want answers, a guide is made available to you through the matching of self-interests. If you desire to know more about science, then a guide who specializes in that area will come forward. If you desire to know about art or music, then an individual who enjoys those areas will be there for you.

You can request a guide of any kind, and they will be available to you. These are individuals who desire to learn and grow from the other side without incarnating at the present moment. They are people, like you, who have life experiences to share. They can be there for you, just as you can be there for another as a physical guide and mentor while you are alive in physical form.

We suggest that you consider interviewing guides before you hire them. There are as many levels of expertise in the guide realm as there are in the physical realm. And if you ask for guidance without being specific, anyone can show up for the job. If you are desperate for help and are unwilling to qualify the applicant, you may end up hiring someone you will not want on your team in the long run.

Remember, it is important to acknowledge the energies you are stringing along with you and take an accounting of what is there. You are God in your realm and it is your prerogative to hire or fire any guide. And it is recommended that you conduct regular reviews of your team so you can be aware of the assistance you currently have available to you.

Sometimes people say they hate their higher selves because they do not appreciate the guidance they have received. We suggest that you receive what you want to receive. It is not the fault of your higher self that you listened to guides who are faulty in their information. It was your decision to hire guidance that is imperfect. Your higher self sits by and allows this to occur because it is within your free will to do so. If you want true guidance, we suggest that you communicate more fully with your higher self, which is that part of you that is wise and connected to Source. Your higher self can determine which guide to hire for which purpose. That support from your higher self is always available.

Question: When you have a gut feeling to do something, can you be receiving direction from your guides rather than your higher self?

Yes. You may think something is intuition, but it is not if it is impure. A gut feeling can be another's energy or a guide leading you in a certain direction. That is why we suggest that you incorporate your higher wisdom into your world through requesting that you stay connected to Source through your higher self. It will bring you wisdom that you know is good for you. Your higher self is there for you at all times when you request it. It is in service to you as your wisdom when you are incarnated in your world.

Question: Do most people have many guides in their space?

165

True, very much so. Your energy space can be filled with a multitude of beings. If you have not held your boundaries, your space can act as a sponge for other energies. This is why you may feel that you have many parts or personalities. The energy that comes through the body may be you, the being who incarnated into the body, your spirit guides, or other energies. When you are talking to someone with many parts, you may ask yourself who you are talking to and truly, you may be addressing a multitude.

Question: Physsie mentioned she wanted to be a guide for us. Do you need to elevate your consciousness to be a guide for another?

No, not at all. When you are on the other side, you can guide another simply through your desire to do so and through their desire to receive your guidance. Then you have an agreement.

There are many instances when individuals cry out in emotional or physical pain seeking guidance. If you are unclear about the level of guidance you want to receive and what your desired outcomes are, then the integrity and purity of that guidance can be questionable. That is why we suggest that you only ask to receive guidance in light and love. Whenever you accept guidance from another, be it someone from this side or the other, it is wise to clarify to yourself and the universe that you accept guidance only through the higher vibrations of light and love.

Question: Can you attract lower level guides if you are less conscious of your desired outcomes?

Yes, and even though you may not be consciously aware of your desires, the guides you attract are most likely aware of their desires. Remember, guides are simply those entities who desire to serve as guides. When a guide desires to serve its own needs through controlling your world, it is of a lower vibration.

Of course, there are also those guides at the middle level who desire to be of pure love, so they do their best to assist you. Their intention is good. They desire to do well but have limited wisdom because their connection to the light of Source is limited.

There are also high level experts from the other side, such as scientists, doctors, engineers, investment advisers, and others who desire to continue their livelihood through assisting you in the physical plane. They are truly experts, and their intentions are also good. But with all of these guides, their own experiences and beliefs may interfere with their purity of thought.

The higher vibration guides hold you in love and assist you in bringing through your light. In its pure form, being a guide is an act of love. In its pure form, a guide is an elevated being who desires to love more and does so by being of service in your world. This is not a codependent relationship, but it is truly a situation of love and adoration. Guidance is simply love incarnating more fully into your world. It is goodness and kindness. The highest vibration of assistance comes from angels, which have nothing but pure love to offer you. But that form of assistance is different from the guidance that is available through spirit guides.

Question: Do guides disconnect at death or do they follow you into your next incarnation?

It all depends on your desire. If you desire to maintain guidance of any kind, it will remain. If you desire to disconnect, it will disconnect. If the guidance finds you less fun on the other side, it can choose to disconnect. Remember, it is a two-way street. Often times, dark guides choose to disengage when you are boring to them and then reconnect if your life becomes more dramatic and interesting. That is why many individual's lives appear to go up and down.

Question: How can you get rid of guides that have less light?

You do so by requesting to disconnect. You do so by saying, "I hereby declare that the agreement I made to allow in all guidance is hereby deemed finished and complete. I disconnect from all guides at this time. Now I only reconnect to those guides who are of light and love and a higher vibration than me and who agree to assist me in my continued enlightenment."

Before you go to bed, you can say to yourself, "I love me. I love every inch of me. I reclaim my body and myself, and I mean it." Commit to this and believe it.

Question: Are there guides that follow family lines through the ages?

True, very much so. When a parent has an agreement and that parent gives birth to a child, it impresses upon the child the design it has for itself. The child then says, "I see. I must accept this guidance. It is a part of my world."

In this way, the agreement is made and passed down generation after generation until a wise individual in the line wakes up and says, "Wait a minute. This is crazy. I do not desire to have that belief. I do not desire to listen to guidance that is faulty. I choose not to." And that individual breaks the agreement for himself and his line or the part of his line that is willing to void the agreement.

For a time, things may go haywire in the life of the one who broke the agreement, for when you say, "I choose to break previous agreements that were made through my family line," lower vibration guidance often chooses not to disconnect from the contract and, instead, comes forward with negotiations. It may say, "It's okay. I will not guide you in the daytime, but I will guide you at night through your dreams. I will back off when things are good, but when things get bad, I will be there to take care of you."

And often you agree to some of the new terms until you realize this is not good and you must break from them too. When the agreements are completely broken, you can walk away and breathe more fully. It may take generations and multiple incarnations to complete this. It could be that your great-great-great-grandfather started to wake up and renegotiate but died before he was complete. He passed on the task to his daughter who said, "Wow, this contract doesn't make sense, but I fear I need protection, so I will keep it." So for many generations it could be hovering above the family line as a permanent fixture until someone chooses to completely break it. It can hover from lifetime to lifetime and incarnation to incarnation as well. Both situations require the same disconnection, whether the agreement is through one individual who incarnates in a variety of places and through a variety of genetic configurations or it is through a genetic line that continues.

A guide can be connected to a genetic line or to an individual (a specific spark of light) who incarnates into a variety of genetic lines. When an individual who has a guide incarnates into a new line, he introduces that guide to that new genetic line. It then becomes a family guide for future generations in that line. Once a guide is introduced into a line it can, and often does, make agreements through time into the past and into the future.

When you pass over, it is best to release all entanglements and disconnect from all guidance, excluding your higher self, whether you consider it to be good or bad. This allows you to see yourself more clearly and make better choices as you move ahead in your awareness. You can always hire more guides in the future and ask that they meet your current needs.

Question: When Anne researched and appreciated her ancestors, she felt she was healing her genetic lines through the ages. Is that right?

True, very much so. She was sprinkling the magic dust of love through her genetic lines so that each individual through whom she incarnated had the opportunity and option to love himself or herself more. That gave them all the possibility to break ties with those energies that are of less light. That was Anne's gift to her world.

Also, many individuals who came in contact with her ancestors were changed as a result of this process. Their options for growth increased through their increased connection with love and light. And Anne also healed herself in past incarnations and touched the lives around her at that time. This is the ripple effect.

Chapter 23

Angels, Archangels, and Guardian Angels

They come to your assistance when you desire it and when you are willing to care for yourself first.

A ngels exist in the fabric of love and hold you in that space so you can love yourself more. Angels support you through love. Archangels also support you through love, just at a stronger level. Guardian angels are there for you as protectors of your whole being—your full self, higher self, and personality. This lasts throughout your earthly experience.

Question: Could you describe angels?

Angels are particles of light that are distributed in your universe to assist you at a high level by being the support that allows for further growth at all levels in your system. They are pure love, and their intention is pure. They come to your assistance when you desire it and when you are willing to care for yourself first. They are not allowed to interfere with you, but if you call on them, they are at the ready. You cannot use them, but they will support you as you better your world.

Angels stand in your vicinity to remind you of love and that you are God, creator in your world. As you proceed with your tasks, you may ask them to assist you in bringing in more light to your creations. They are not meant to be your mentors, but they are meant to show you what love is. If you desire to truly know love, ask the angels to teach you. The angelic realm will come forward, surround you, and vibrate that feeling of love so you can mimic it and feel it yourself.

Question: Could you further describe angels?

Angels are those beings of light who desire to move ahead through assisting others. They come to your aid when you desire it and when it is in your highest good. If you say to yourself, "I need someone to fix my relationship with my boyfriend because I do not want to do it myself," then the angels will hold back, for that is not their duty. They are not your servants.

Angels are beings of light who come forward to support you when you love yourself more. They are like wings beneath your feet in that they allow you to elevate yourself and feel yourself as more whole when you have a strong desire to do that but have difficulty feeling it yourself. You could see angels as supporters of the fabric of love who are there to assist you in accessing more love for yourself. That is their role. They desire to be acknowledged as a support team when you request their assistance.

Angels are no better or worse than you are. They are not to be thought of as angels of light who are here to save you, for that is untrue. They are not your saviors. Instead, they are your supporters when you love yourself more, desire more love, and are in communication with your higher self.

It is like trying to drive your car to the top of a hill. That is your desire and intention. The angels will help push you that last mile because you are already moving ahead in your chosen direction under your own mobility. They offer you that final oomph when you need it, but they will not otherwise interfere.

Question: What is the role of an angel?

Each one has different attributes and, therefore, assumes different roles. They come when requested. You may see an angel "attached" to an individual who continuously prays to that angel, but that is not the intention of the setup. When you call on a specific angel all the time, it is as if you freeze what should be freely moving. The angelic realm is fluid. It is not meant to be static or grabbed onto. Angels are not meant to be solidified.

You could see angels as sparks of light held in love that come forward as ideas or information meant to assist you in moving ahead. These ideas are always brought forward through creativity and love. If you curse the world with hatred while calling on the angels to help you when you are dying, they will hold back because they are only able to come forward in love.

When you are disgruntled with yourself, the angelic realm cannot come forward because there is no match in vibration there. When you criticize yourself or another, you drop your energy to a level that is much darker than they are, so they have no entry into your realm because they would disrupt you too much with their light. But if you say to yourself for just a moment, "I love myself," then for that moment there is an entrée, and they can come forward as a thought for you to be more loving to yourself. That thought leads you to take action and make movement, which brings about the possibility that they can be more available to you.

Remember, when you begin to walk in a positive direction, they stand behind you and beside you as your support. Your

173

positive actions increase your vibration, which attracts other loving beings to you and loving actions out of those around you. Therefore, your reality changes. Your actions bring about miracles.

Miracles are not a mystery. Your positive actions increase the vibration in your field and your energy system becomes filled with sparks of light and love for yourself that attract more light and love around you. This creates a field of energy that brings forward your desires if those desires are in love and light. If your desires are in darkness, then again, the angels cannot assist you because their energy is too light to match that, so there is no entrée.

As an example, let us say that you desire to have a puppy because you feel that would open your heart and be of benefit to the puppy. The angels then walk behind you and beside you to assist you in finding a puppy. As you walk down the sidewalk contemplating that you would like a puppy, the energy of light held in love calls out to all the puppies in the neighborhood to come down to the sidewalk to see you. The puppies greet you, and you say to yourself, "Look, there are so many puppies. I wonder which one might be available and appropriate for me to take home?"

By asking that question of the universe, the puppy who is meant to be with you comes forward and makes himself known. And because you are supported by love and surrounded by the sparks of light from the angelic realm, the owner of the puppy feels the urge to come out of his house and ask you if you might be able to take that puppy off his hands because he has too many dogs. He says, "Would you take this puppy home with you? It would be our pleasure to give him to you." It is complete, so the angels retreat because that job has been well done.

Then the next time you need assistance, you remember this example and bring it forward in your being to support yourself more. In this way, you become your own angelic force. You become your own creator in your world and self-supporter in love. The goal of the angelic realm is to assist you in remembering that you are God in your realm. Angels assist you in raising your vibration once you are willing to raise it yourself.

Question: Do Angels have personalities?

Yes. All beings have character, or an energy signature, specific to that being. When your uniqueness cries out and becomes a spark of light in the universe, you let go and become a unique being held in the fabric of love. That is part of the experience. From your level of personality desiring to understand angels, it may be difficult to see differences in their personalities because you are interpreting them from a limited perspective. As your filters of interpretation drop away, you will become more able to see the subtle differences and appreciate them more fully.

Question: Can humans become angels?

Angels are energies, or configurations of light particles. They vibrate at a higher level than you do and they are closer to Source. They are not a part of your makeup in your reality, but they support you. You cannot be an angel, and an angel cannot be you. Angels are a different configuration of energy, but in the larger scheme of things, you are all one, for you all emanate from Source.

Question: How do angels communicate?

Because angels vibrate much higher than you do, their communication with you is telepathic. They have no physical bodies, but they can choose to appear in your world as a conglomeration of energies that supports you. You could see this as the appearance of an etheric body, which then disappears. This appearance would only occur if you had been requesting assistance and were truly in need of confirmation. Otherwise, the experience would be purely telepathic, and you would feel the emanation of support around you if you asked to experience it.

Question: Could you explain further how miracles happen with angels?

When you get around the vibration of a higher being, you emanate more love yourself because your vibration rises in response to the activation of love in your system. When this occurs, you are more connected to the grid, or fabric, of love, which allows more life force energy to flow through you. This allows you to attract those things you desire more quickly. Becoming closer to your higher self also increases the level of your vibration.

You must attribute goodness to yourself for doing this. To increase the number of miracles in your world, ask to be cleaned out and connected to Source, and appreciate the angelic realm. In turn, they will appreciate you and hang around you more. If you have pure thoughts and love in your heart, you will vibrate more similarly to angels, and they will be able to raise your vibration by being in your vicinity. They have no access to you when you are darker and of a much lower vibration that is too dissimilar to their own vibrations.

Question: What are archangels?

Archangels are a conglomeration of beings, or sparks of light, that focus energy in a particular direction. They have a greater energy stream and support ability than angels. You could see them as an amplification of light. When an angel desires to create energy of great magnitude, it combines its energies with another angel to increase the strength and power of light.

Question: Are archangels a combination of angels?

True, very much so. Originally, when a task or cause of interest exhibited itself in the universe, certain angels came forward desiring to be part of the effort to bring forward light in a certain vibration. When their interests were similar, they coalesced and combined their lights. Over time, this combination became identified as a single angel, or archangel, with a name to it. However, it truly is a conglomeration of beings of like interest and desire that has coalesced more completely over time.

You may think that this combination of energies remains constant, but it does not. When an angel says to itself, "For a while, I would like to experience what it is like to look over the fairy kingdom rather than the human kingdom," then that angel releases its hold on the conglomeration of angelic beings and shifts to look after the fairy kingdom. This allows another angel to enter the archangel vibration, which is held for the originally desired task. There is as a nucleus formed around an interest, and everything is in constant motion.

Question: After my (Greg's) first wife died, I called upon Archangel Michael for help. Is Michael real or just a thought form?

It is both. The qualities you desired of strength and protection came forward as Michael when you desired assistance. However, when you told yourself you could not move ahead alone, you became lonely and your energy dropped with this idea that you were incomplete. This caused a disconnection from the actual being and an accessing of the thought form, or the condensed energies of thoughts that had taken on the form of Michael over time. For you to receive the bounty of the energy of Archangel Michael, you had to be willing to come forward with strength on your own. When you did this, you could feel the support that was truly there for you. When you wanted another to rescue you, the support would drop away again and you would be in contact with the thought form.

As for the reality of Archangel Michael, you could say it is a configuration of angelic beings that come forward in a construct to allow you to recognize it as such. It is a constantly moving experience that is light in nature.

Archangel Michael can also be considered a thought form. As many people pray to be rescued by a greater being, their belief that they can be saved grows and coalesces into a thought form you would also call Michael, though it would not be the real thing. This thought form develops further as energies of lesser light are drawn to the situation where people pray for assistance from their inner place of lack. We do not suggest praying to this lesser experience of Michael.

Question: So is the true energy of Archangel Michael a conglomeration of angelic beings?

True, very much so. Nothing is truly singular. All things are a configuration of light according to desire, and the desire of Archangel Michael is to be all encompassing in strength and love. It is like a powerhouse of energy that draws upon many realms of existence for support. While angels are more singular in their vibration, archangels are more of a conglomeration of angelic beings that desire to create a more dramatic affect.

178

Question: Would this be the same for Archangel Raphael and others?

When you create a construct of an archangel, you draw on the idea that it contains more strength than normal. Therefore, your construct requires more angels of light to come forward as a conglomeration of beings to create this effect. That is your request, and by their choice, they do so. They stand as one but they are many.

Question: What is a guardian angel?

A guardian angel is your interpretation of the energy that supports you, as a whole, as you move through life. It is energy from the angelic realm that supports you in your human experience. It is truly the love that holds you in your universe as exhibited through an energy system of light that is identified for the protection of your being as you traverse your world. It is not meant to interfere. It cannot interfere according to the stipulations of universal law, but it can be there for you. So as you grow, you can request assistance and receive it. You could see your guardian angel as backup support for your higher self and personality in your realm of creating.

Question: Does everyone have a guardian angel?

You could see it as one guardian angel per personality even though it is more like one guardian angel per full self. Your full self has one angel that is there for you. That angel is more responsible for you than others. You could say that this guardian angel is specific to your full self, and your full self has many emanations in life. Therefore, that guardian angel would be specific to all those emanations. The guardian angel is non-specific to space and time, so it can reside in many places at once.

As you desire more support, more support is available to you through the angelic realm. You can call upon the angelic realm at any time to assist you. But they will only support you in the direction that you have chosen. They will never interfere. Think of your guardian angel as a hammock that is available for you to lie in to rest. That hammock is always available to you so you may sleep, dream, and remember that you are whole, you are God. It is your support.

We suggest that your true guardian angel should be named your higher self. That is the one who is responsible for you and looks after you as an individual. You could say that the guardian angel looks after the full self and the higher self looks after the personality.

Heaven

*You remember who you are, which
is a being of light existing in love
and having an experience.*

Over the years, heaven has been researched using hypnotic regressions, psychic accounts, and near death experiences. There have been many similarities in the reports, and the differences have been understandable given that we interpret everything we see though our own beliefs and filters. Ultimately, heaven will be an experience of self-discovery unique to each of us because our perspectives are uniquely our own.

What is heaven? It could be described as a resting place for the weary traveler. It is a construct that exists, but it can be altered according to your beliefs and desires. As you heal yourself more, you benefit from your increased awareness and see more of what it truly is.

Question: Could you describe heaven?

Heaven is that configuration of energies that is available to you as a resting place while you recuperate and adjust your energies to receive more light. You could see it as hovering above your world in another vibrational field that is subtler than Earth but not too distant. It is not far from your reality of Earth for it is connected to it. It is part of the setup for your experience here.

Another way to see it is as a floating amoeba slightly above your planet. It is like a cloud of energy that is somewhat pink in nature, meaning that it holds love and support for you. People who pass over to the other side enter this reality of heaven in their etheric form. The reality you call heaven unfolds for them depending on their belief systems. Just as you migrate to places on Earth where you feel most comfortable, so do you pick out areas in heaven that feel most comfortable to you. It is no different from Earth in this way.

The difference is that you are in etheric form rather than physical form. The density level is less, so you create more easily with your ideas. In physical reality it takes the additional step of bringing something into form after you have had the idea of creating it.

Question: So is it more of a resting place than a destination?

True, very much so. It is a place of recuperation in a realm that is connected to Earth and where there is a returning of light to your system. It is like a way station, for you can move on from there. You can incarnate into other lives to have other experiences or you can choose to move on to subtler realms beyond heaven. It vibrates in a density that is less dense than Earth but denser than other realms.

Question: How would you describe heaven in simpler terms?

Heaven is a way station. It is like a gas station in the middle of a long road where you stop to fuel up, pick up food and maps, and get your bearings. From heaven, you decide where you would like to go next. It is a stop on your journey rather than the destination.

Question: So heaven is place to recuperate?

Heaven is a place of rest and recuperation. However, the idea that you must recuperate is faulty. As you move ahead, your being, or sense of self, evolves to the point that you take care of yourself better as you move along in life. When you do this, there is less need for down time, because you give yourself love as you go. You fill a need as it occurs to you, so there is less need to be filled through recuperation time in heaven. The goal is to care for yourselves on a continuous basis to maintain your being with ease.

When you as a personality choose to separate from your higher self, which has access to Source, love is minimized, as is the flow of light. When this occurs, your being requires recuperation. You could say that you are strangling yourself, your lower self, by keeping it from the air when you are lacking in love and light. This often happens when you incarnate.

If you dove under the water and held your breath for a time, you would eventually have to come to the surface to breathe. Breathing is what you could say you do when you go to heaven to recuperate. You reestablish the flow within your system. You activate your cells and bring them back to life.

If you can believe in yourself and love who you are, there is no oxygen starvation. Everything is in flow all the time. You remain at the surface breathing or you take a breathing device with you when you dive down and enter other realms of experience. You remember who you are, which is a being of light existing in love and having an experience.

We suggest that you look at yourself as having this as a possibility. If you do so now, you will require less sleep and less dreamtime, for you will be accessing your wisdom as you remain more awake. The light flows through your system as you hold yourself in love. When this occurs, you also forgo the need for death.

Death is a concept that allows you downtime to recuperate when you have held your breath—separated from Source—for so long. When separation occurs, you must gasp for air and stay on the surface of the water for a time until you can breathe normally again. Heaven, as you currently conceive it, is that place of recuperation where you are loved and held in love and where the light shines around you, filling you with wonderful ideas. When love is constant and you feel fulfilled, the light can flow through you and bring you ideas of beauty and goodness that you desire to fulfill. You fulfill your desires, for there is no lack.

We suggest that you create heaven on Earth for yourself at this time. Life would be more fulfilling for you if you did this. Rather than saying, "Oh, I must wait until I die, and then I shall have everything I desire. It will be beautiful, and I will sit at the right hand of God," we suggest that you become the creator yourself, now, in life.

Question: Are there levels of heaven?

There are levels, or neighborhoods, in heaven just as there are levels of anything else. You gravitate toward those areas that are most like you. If your level of awareness is minimal, then your heaven will vibrate lower than the heaven of those who are quite elevated in their being. It is like going to a school that has kindergarten through twelfth grade. There are children in every grade level. Everyone is in the same school but those in different grade levels are separated from each other. All the students are to be appreciated no matter what their level of learning.

Question: *Most people report feeling bliss when they get to the other side, but Physsie did not. What is the difference?*

The cloud you walk through to get to the other side is a field of energy that allows you to let go of negativity in your system, be at one with All That Is, and feel bliss. When Physsie looked in her heart and saw the jewel of her light there, she was already in that bliss-like state. She did not need to go through the repatterning of energy to release negativity at that time. That release often brings about the experience of bliss.

You could say that Physsie crossed over prepared. She loved herself more before she went through the cloudy door. Therefore, she did not experience a significant increase in love or bliss during her passage. Most people do not cross over as prepared as Physsie was and forget to look into their own hearts for love. They go from a less loving negative state to one of much love and bliss, which makes for a significant contrast and euphoric state.

Question: *Could Physsie describe heaven for us?*

Physsie says, "They call this heaven, but it's not what I thought it would be. It is an entryway. It is where you go to love yourself more for a time. It heals you of old wounds so you can continue. It is where you design your reality.

"The people here make you feel loved so that love is all you feel. This allows you to love yourself more, and once you love yourself more, you have the energy to move ahead. The love wakes you up. Then you can be curious again and want to go somewhere. Otherwise, you don't have the idea to move ahead—and ideas move you. Without an idea, a curiosity, or a desire you stay the same, there is no movement. When you get an idea, you go wherever you want, and there are no limits.

"Also, you should know that it's not solid here, it's moveable. When you think a thought, things change to match your thought. It can be one way one day and another way the next. It's not like other realities. It's fluid. It is made up of ideas, but moveable ones, not solid ones. They can change shape, and then your reality does too."

Question: Physsie, what would you like for your life design on the other side?

"As for what I'd like to do with my design of reality, I think I'd like to have dogs. They are such loving beings. I don't need people as much as I'd like dogs. And rabbits. I'd like rabbits. But they should be separated from the dogs, of course, until they become friends. Also, I'd like flowers. They are so pretty with so many colors. And a wall. I'd like to build a rock wall to keep out the goats. Goats roam around here. I've seen them. Some people like goats, so I want to put limits on my garden so it's just for me and not the goats.

"Now I have to go. I need to sleep and dream some more things into reality. And by the way, the sky is so blue here."

Question: How can we create heaven on Earth?

You are the creator in your realm. You are a snapshot of Source. Source is within you and all around you. Source is you having an experience. Therefore, take it upon yourself to have an experience now rather than putting it off until you reach that place you call heaven.

If you believe you can create such goodness on Earth, then you will transform your experience. You will give yourself all those things you desire at this time, and all will be good. Then there is no need for heaven because you have created it within yourself and have produced it in your world. This reality is meant to be in your world. You are not meant to wait for anything, for that is a sign of lack. You are meant to have and create whatever you desire in an instant with the full flow of light that is held in the arms, or fabric, of love.

When you allow yourself to create heaven, which is all your desires fulfilled on Earth, then there is no longer the need for death. Death is the separation from life as you conceptualize it. When you receive your desires at all times, there is no separation. There is no having it only in heaven while not having it on Earth. Instead, you are in constant flow. It is the raising up of your energies to allow you to believe in yourself and create a world that includes love and the flow of light to completion.

Appendix A

Energy Exercises

You are here on Earth to experience, expand, and grow—to increase your vibration, to ascend to higher densities. This means cleaning out old beliefs, thoughts, ideas, experiences, and energies that no longer serve you. The more you clean out in the physical realm, where you collected these energies, the easier your transition is and the more options you have on the other side. These energy exercises, when practiced regularly, can help you achieve your goals.

Ground, Define Your Space, and Connect to Source

The goal of this exercise is to clear your space and be more present, focused, and intuitive. You ground your body to the earth, define your energy space, which creates a receptacle to receive light, and connect to the light of Source. This is a clearing and connecting process in three steps: (1) ground your body, (2) set your space by creating an energy bubble around you, and (3) connect to Source through your tube of light to receive pure light.

Ground

In the past, meditation techniques generally took you out of your body to explore the universe. This gave you the experience of moving beyond your physical body, which was important at that time. But when you are out there, less of your energy and consciousness is here. So the goal now is to bring in more of your spirit to your body. The more of your spirit that is in your body, the more energy you have here to create what you want.

Grounding is important because in this modern age we are more involved in ungrounded activities, such as being inside buildings and working with electronics. Being in a natural environment grounds you and naturally releases energy toxins from your system. If you are alive in this physical reality, you are already somewhat grounded to it, but the more you choose to purposefully ground, the more powerful you become.

Here is the process:

1) You can do this process standing or lying down, though it is easiest to begin by sitting upright in a chair with your feet flat on the floor. You may also go outside, put your bare feet in the grass, and ground from there.

2) Imagine you are sitting on a grounding tube that goes all the way from the base of your spine down to the center of the earth. Also imagine smaller tubes that go from the bottom of your feet to the center of Earth.

3) Once these tubes are connected, imagine turning on your grounding tube as if you were turning on the disposal in your sink. You are grinding out old energies to the center of the earth where they are recycled.

4) Rather than using effort, let it happen easily. You can imagine yourself as an hourglass that is turned over. The sand naturally flows out with gravity.

Define Your Space

Next, you need to define your energy space, or aura, so that you have a manageable realm within which to create. Your aura is the energy emanation from your chakras that encompasses

190

your body like a cloud. By defining your space, you give yourself a healthy boundary, or energy bubble. This also creates a vessel to receive your light.

Some people believe that your aura should be as big as possible, but that allows everyone to walk through your space. It is hard to manage your space when it is large. Plus, whenever you feel like it, you can always expand and contract your energy field.

Here is the process:

1) Imagine you are pulling in your aura cloud to arm's length from your body.

2) With your arms stretched out, turn your fingers in towards you with the intention of defining your aura. You can imagine touching the edge of a clear plexiglass shield that encircles you.

3) Swing your arms to your right, to your left, and above your head. Imagine that your arms are also swinging below your feet. You are creating a clear egg-like bubble all around you that is arm's length out. You have now created your defined space, or energy bubble.

4) Notice how this protects you from the outside environ ment and outside energies, just as a well-constructed building would do.

5) On the inside, you can now create an environment that is both enjoyable and useful for the collecting the light that you bring in from Source.

Connect to Source

Once you have grounded and defined your space, connect more fully to Source and bring in your light. As an energy being, you naturally have a tube of light to Source that brings you life force energy and intuition. By putting your attention on your tube, purposefully connecting to Source, and visualizing a strong connection, you can bring in more of your light.

The light that you bring down this tube is your own unique light signature. You are like a snowflake—your tube and your light are unique to you. When you incarnate, you do not always bring enough of your light with you. At other times, your tube to Source can become clogged with faulty ideas that you are not good enough, or that you are incomplete. So it is important to choose to clean out your tube and bring in enough light to support you fully.

You can ask your higher self to monitor this and ensure that you are bringing in the right amount of light at any particular time. You may need only a trickle, or you may need a stream. The goal of this process is to clean out your energy system and bring more of you into your body. As you bring in more of your light, you are able to create more fully in your world.

Here is the process:

1) Imagine a gold central sun, ball of light, or Source above your head.

2) Take your consciousness there and connect with that energy.

3) See a tube coming down from this central sun to the top of your head. This may feel like putting on a crown or a top hat. It secures your connection to Source.

4) Imagine golden light flowing through the tube to you, filling in your body and your bubble. You are filling in all the places that are empty from grounding out old energies.

5) Let go of the excess by having it flow down your grounding tube to the center of the earth.

6) Let it flow naturally. Let it happen.

Grounding, Defining Your Space, and Connecting to Source

After you do this exercise, notice how you feel lighter with less "junk" in your space. Your thoughts may be clearer. You may notice more energy in your system. This process can also stir up some emotions as you are cleaning out, so be gentle with yourself. Take walks in nature, enjoy the sunshine, rest, bathe, and drink plenty of water.

Call Back Your Energy

The goal of this exercise is to call back your energy so you can be more present and powerful, as well as enjoy yourself more. While you are alive, you can call back energy you have sent to people, places, and things. By doing this, you can decrease the time spent in recuperation on the other side.

Through your intention to be whole and your love of self, you are able to call back your energy. All That Is stated in the text, "Feel yourself being fully whole and present where you are now. Appreciate and enjoy your current situation. Through enjoyment, you call back your energy, because to enjoy yourself, you must be present. Then laugh at yourself and your situation, because laughter brings to you a vibration that reverberates throughout your being and calls you home. It ripples through your system. It is a sound that calls you home."

Here is the process:

1) Each day as you awaken, ask yourself, "How can I be more present today?"

2) Be open and listen to receive an intuitive answer.

3) Then say, "I choose to be present. I choose to focus in each moment. I now call back the parts of me that were on a

mental vacation. I choose to focus now. I feel good about this. I give thanks that I am present. I am whole."

Release Negativity

The goal of this exercise is to release negativity from your space so you can be more fully yourself and feel better. Negativity naturally releases when you see yourself as a stronger container of love and bring in more light.

Here is the process:

1) Be aware that you have negativity in some form in your system.

2) Decide to release the negativity.

3) On a daily basis, choose to have loving thoughts towards yourself and others. Choose to lessen your criticisms and instead, be discerning. This choice to love yourself naturally releases negativity from your system.

4) Engage in activities that bring you joy every day.

5) Choose to see yourself as whole—you need nothing from the outside to make you whole because you are whole from within. As All That Is stated in the text, "To release negativity you must see yourself as whole. You cannot see yourself as incomplete and expect completion to begin. This is a requirement. So if you see yourself as complete, as good as you are, then your abilities to move ahead are increased. Wholeness must be considered first. Then the energy of lack releases, for it is no longer necessary and it no longer has a place in your system."

6) Choose to bring in more light. "Each time you see negativity coming towards you, choose the light." Negativity will automatically release from your system because lesser light beings must give up their claim to greater light.

7) Choose to love yourself more during your sleep. You can set your intention to love yourself more while you sleep with the assistance of your higher self. When you love yourself more, you claim your space as your dominion and take ownership of your being. When you love yourself more, you have the ability to bring in more light and be more present as yourself.

8) Before you go to sleep, say to yourself, "I love me. I love every inch of me. I reclaim my body and myself. And, I mean it."

Disconnect from Guides with Less Light

The goal of this exercise is to disconnect you from old guides so you can choose again and stay current. You may have enrolled some spirit guides who are no longer appropriate for you. They could be from your childhood, your last life, or your ancestors. Because you accepted them at some point, you give thanks for them and let them know you simply desire to move ahead on your own or with new guides.

You can use this process to disconnect from guides who have less light and less consciousness and rebuild who you are connected with. Ask your higher self to assist you.

Here is the process:

Request to disconnect from guides with less light by saying the following to yourself: "I hereby declare that the agreement I made to allow in all guidance is hereby deemed finished and complete. At this time, I disconnect from all guides. I now reconnect with only those guides of a higher vibration of light and love. I ask that they assist me in my growth, enlightenment, and achievements."

Become More Intuitive

For exercises on how to become more intuitive in your daily life, we highly recommend our book, *Eureka! Understanding and Using the Power of Your Intuition*, and our *Intuitive Skills* series of CD courses. Visit *GoIntuition.com* for more information.

Appendix B

Key Words and Phrases

The following key words and phrases are from conversations with All That Is. They are taken from this book as well as our previous book, *The Path of Intuition: Your Guidebook for Life's Journey.*

All That Is

The whole of All That Is is that which emanates from Source and is in all things. All That Is, which communicates with Anne, is a loving group consciousness of nonphysical energy beings that comes from a place far from our general experience. They say about themselves: "We are you. We are no different. We are All That Is."

Angels

Angels are particles of light that are distributed in your universe to assist you at a high level by being the support that allows for further growth at all levels in your system. They are pure love, and their intention is pure. They come to your assistance when you desire it and when you are willing to care for yourself first. They are not allowed to interfere with you, but if you call on them, they are at the ready. You cannot use them, but they will support you as you better your world.

Angels stand in your vicinity to remind you of love and that you are God, creator in your world. As you proceed with your tasks, you may ask them to assist you in bringing in more light to your creations. They are not meant to be your mentors, but they are meant to show you what love is. If you desire to truly know love, ask the angels to teach you. The angelic realm will come forward, surround you, and vibrate that feeling of love so you can mimic it and feel it yourself.

Ascension

Ascension is the returning of subtle energies, or higher vibrations, to your system, which allows you to grow. Ascension is not a magical process. It is a necessary process to shift dimensions, or densities. It is the raising up of your energies to allow you to believe in yourself and create a reality that includes love and the flow of light to completion.

Beliefs

Beliefs are habitual patterns of thinking. You have an experience and make a judgment about it in the form of a thought. And as you continue to think that thought, it becomes engrained in your energy system as a belief. These beliefs can be positive and supportive of your growth or negative and non-affirming of who you are as an independent, creative being, and they can be adopted from your parents, culture, or religion. They bring about the creation of form in your world.

Death

Death is a concept that allows you downtime to recuperate when you have held your breath—separated from Source—for so long. The light flows through your system as you hold yourself in love. When this occurs, you forgo the need for death.

Full Self, Spirit, Soul, Essence

Your full self, or spirit, is all of you, your existence. It encompasses your entire being. It includes those aspects of you that are not reachable from the physical realm.

Your full self is the light that is specific to you. It is your full emanation of spirit that is distinct in the emanation of light. It encompasses all of your bodies and your energy. Your higher self, in contrast, is that aspect of your full self, or spirit, with which you can communicate from your physical form.

God in Your Realm

You could say that you are God, creator in your realm, your universe, your world, your reality. Everything around you is your creation. Each level of existence within you, such as the cells within your body, experiences itself as creator. The stream of experience is non-ending.

Source, the creator who created you, was embraced by love in order to create. Now, you, God creator in your universe, must hold love for yourself. You must experience that sense of forgiveness, acceptance, and appreciation for yourself and others so that you, too, can create. These aspects are required for the love to hold the light, which brings about creation, the ignited spark, at any level of experience. (See also Source.)

Heaven

Heaven is that configuration of energies that is available to you as a resting place while you recuperate and adjust your energies to receive more light. It is like a way station, for you can move on from there.

However, the idea that you must recuperate is faulty. As you move ahead, your being, or sense of self, evolves to the point that you take care of yourself better as you move along in life. When you do this, there is less need for down time, because you give yourself love as you go. You fill a need as it occurs to you, so there is less need to be filled through recuperation time in heaven. The goal is to care for yourselves on a continuous basis to maintain your being with ease.

Higher Self

When you, as a personality, incarnate into a physical body of your choosing, you leave behind a part of you in a higher vibration. This is your higher self. You could say that it remains in spirit so you can maintain perspective in your world of form. This gives you a fighting chance in the world you call "reality." Your higher self is there for you when you mess up and look for better answers. It is your best friend because it is your access to higher wisdom, your connection to Source. It has your highest good at heart and has nothing else to do but be there for you. It is you from a higher perspective.

Intention

Intention is your desire to be a certain way. It defines who you are. It is the defining of desire that allows for the creation in form of your desires. Intention is you being the creative spark of light in form, which you are.

Intuition

Simply stated, intuition is your access to Source, the Source of All That Is. Intuition is the aspect of you that descends as light particles in the column (which you could see as a beam or tube) of light to feed you information from Source. There must first be the request, because your intuition is set up to receive questions. These requests feed up the tube, so to say, as light particles through your higher self to your full self and on to Source. Source, or that grand being above you in creation, feeds back answers to your questions and requests. It is a feedback loop.

Life Force Energy

Life force energy is the energy that comes down the tube of light with intuition to fill your body with light. It is on a mission from Source to ignite every cell in your body and bring your body life. This life force energy is information that is available to you at any time when you are ready to receive it. It is similar to intuition in that it feeds your body with life and all the answers you need at any time.

Light

Within the light is intuition and life force energy that feeds your body and mind with all the information you need to continue to grow and expand with every thought. Thoughts are of the light. They are of creation. When you hold love for yourself as you fill your body with light, you allow yourself to expand in the light even further. The goal is to have your physical body filled with light.

Love

Love is the backdrop of all things. It is the petri dish to which you add the substance of light so that you may grow and evolve. It has no beginning and no end. It is the fabric, the deep velvetiness, or void, of space that holds love for you. It awaits your spark of light to enter its vastness, and then the further light that follows, to give birth to your experience.

Loving Yourself

The idea is to love yourself more. As you do so, your higher self, or that aspect of you that is wise and has access to Source, drops further into your reality and brings you more wisdom, more intuition. As this occurs, you experience more light moving throughout your whole system. You experience more life force energy flowing through you, which activates your cells. As this occurs, the nucleus of each entity or cell can give birth as well, and on and on it continues. As this occurs, you have access to more and more information.

The more you love yourself, the more you forgive yourself and others for the past, the more you enjoy and appreciate who you are, the wider the expanse of love is within your system. This allows your light to expand. If you can love yourself more, you can double, triple or quadruple the available experiences for yourself because you have increased the container of love that can then receive more light, which, in turn, brings about even more experiences.

This is why focusing on loving yourself is the number one priority. Just as love came first in the universe, so is it for you in your universe. If you focus on love, loving yourself in your universe, appreciating who you are, forgiving yourself, and giving thanks for being love, you can then focus on creating. What do you desire? Once you know your desire, you ignite that spark of light and have an experience. If you decide you do not like that particular experience, you simply collapse the light in that area, move on, and create again. That is the microcosm and the macrocosm of creating.

Lower Self, Personality

Your personality, or lower self, is that part of you that includes the challenges you have had throughout your experiences. Your experience could be defined as lifetimes or nonlinear simultaneous experiences. These experiences act as feedback that keeps coming back to you until you receive specific learnings. You, as your higher self, deemed these learnings to be important for you to move through in order to return to the light, or the subtler emanation of spirit.

When you incarnate you take a part of yourself, a droplet of who you are, and drop it into the physical body you created for yourself. When you do this, your physical body comes to life. It is part of your personality, or lower self.

The lower self that incarnates is responsible for that incarnation. It is allowed to act freely through free will and, therefore, must tend to itself. The higher self is there to assist the lower self in gaining understanding and wisdom about how to maneuver well through this world. But, ultimately, it is the responsibility of the lower self to clean up after its incarnation.

As you start connecting more to the whole of who you are, your lower self (less wise self, more dense self, ego, personality self) desires to connect more with your higher self, and that integrates your personality. When you do this, you have more access to Source.

Source

Source is the grand creator for your world. It is the expansiveness that is reaching out into the universe to experience itself. So, as your parent, let us say, Source guides you and allows you to have access to wisdom that is beyond your realm of experience. If you ask for help, Source is an available teacher for you. If you do not ask, nothing is offered. Source is:

- Born in love.
- The nucleus of the light.

- The center of your existence.
- The life-giving force that puts forth light.
- The creating device that goes out as light to experience itself as life.
- The beginning and ending of life.
- What you experience as the grand creator.
- The grander expression of who you are.
- Your parent. You are the children of Source, the children of the light held in love.
- Its own experience.

Spirit Guides

Spirit guides are individuals who come forward as volunteers to assist you in making decisions in your life. If you have questions and want answers, a guide is made available to you through the matching of self-interests. If you desire to know more about science, then a guide who specializes in that area will come forward. If you desire to know about art or music, then an individual who enjoys those areas will be there for you.

Thought Forms

Thought forms are thoughts you and others have released into the ether like pollution that gathers with similar thoughts into a cloud of energy that floats through your reality.

Wholeness

Wholeness is experienced through knowing you are God as that continuation of light from Source that has no beginning or end in your realm. You may feel somewhat separate in this earth experience, but any separation is an illusion. The experience of separation is granted for each life experience so you may learn who you are as God, creator in your realm. Truly, you are part of the original light, and as such you are whole.

To summarize, you are part of Source, the whole that experiences your world as love and light. Source emanates light, and you are a spark of light. You are connected to Source through that tube of light, which holds intuition and life force energy within it. To fully function as a being, you must attribute goodness to yourself and experience yourself as whole as part of Source held in love.

Appreciation

We would like to thank All That Is, **Physsie Salisbury**, Lewis Bostwick (founder, Berkeley Psychic Institute), and others on the other side who telepathically communicated with us about the journey to heaven. We have learned so much about life and the afterlife and we now know how to improve our transitioning, recuperation, and life on the other side through the actions we take today.

Our clients motivated us to bring this information forward through their continued questioning about loved ones on the other side. Family and friends helped us clarify this material through their readings. Our editor, Melanie Mulhall (Dragonheart), and designer, Nick Zelinger (NZ Graphics), attended to the meaning and details of this work with impeccability.

Our heartfelt thanks goes to Penncy Peirce for her insightful and moving foreword. It brought me (Anne) to tears, and I work with people who have passed all the time.

Our deepest gratitude goes to those who endorsed this book with such thoughtful words. It is a joy to live in a community with such inner-focused companions.

We have already started our next book in which we further explore heaven, and we hope you will join us on this continued exploration of the inner worlds. This book is dedicated to you, our readers and friends, who seek a deeper understanding of both sides of the veil.

About the Authors

Anne Salisbury, PhD, MBA is an intuitive (clairvoyant), hypnotherapist, psychotherapist, and business consultant who helps her clients find answers to questions about relationships, the workplace, health issues, and life's journey. Anne holds advanced degrees in psychology and finance and a BFA in fine art.

In the 1970s Anne embraced meditation and by the 1980s she was trained in hypnotherapy, intuitive skills and dream work. After leaving a Fortune 500 career in the 1990s she founded the Transpersonal Hypnotherapy Institute, which has certified thousands in hypnotherapy and intuition techniques. Her awareness was further expanded through her time spent in India with the Dalai Lama and Mother Teresa. Since she was a child, Anne has connected with the loving group consciousness, which calls itself "All That Is." She has professionally channeled this intuitive wisdom since 2004.

Greg Meyerhoff is an intuitive business consultant, intuition trainer, coach, and speaker. He helps clients and businesses break through energy blocks to experience success with greater clarity and ease.

In 1975, Greg started his practice with Transcendental Meditation and the TM-Sidhi program. After receiving his degree in business management from the University of South Florida, he applied his intuition to sales. He spent two decades as a senior account executive and received the highest company awards for his intuitive sales techniques. Greg then expanded his intuitive work to animals, and in 1997 he led group dolphin interactions in the Caribbean. He has enjoyed working with many species of animals since then.

The company, Go Intuition, Inc., was founded in 2000 and focuses on intuitive business consulting, coaching, energy clearing/feng shui, pet psychic readings, and communications with loved ones who have crossed over to the other side. As cofounders Anne and Greg also invite you to personally witness channelings with the higher wisdom of All That Is during which time you can ask questions. Additionally, they have volunteered their time as the pet psychics for the Summit County Animal Shelter.

As a married couple, Anne and Greg developed the *Eureka System*™, which they teach nationwide and internationally. This system is described in the 2008 book, *Eureka! Understanding and Using the Power of Your Intuition*. Their second award-winning, best-selling book, *The Path of Intuition: Your Guidebook for Life's Journey*, features deeper insights into intuitive wisdom. They are based in Colorado where they enjoy hiking, skiing, and the inspiring wildlife. Their services are available to you in person and by phone worldwide.

For more information on any of their books or to schedule sessions, visit their website *GoIntuition.com*.

Anne and Greg always appreciate hearing from you and learning about how this book has helped you.

Learn More

Bring Intuition into Your Organization

Anne Salisbury and Greg Meyerhoff are available for entertaining results-oriented speeches, seminars, and trainings on intuition.

Receive Intuitive Information

Where do you want to be this time next year? Receive intuitive consulting, coaching, and energy clearing/feng shui in person and by phone to gain clarity on relationships, business, health, pets, and loved ones who have crossed over.

Develop Your Psychic Abilities

Increase your ability to access intuition with comprehensive distance learning intuitive skills courses. You can achieve amazing results: decrease stress, increase focus, improve your decision making ability, and tap into your intuitive abilities.

Free Audio Downloads

Download free audios of conversations with All That Is and self-hypnosis scripts that help you access your intuition. Learn how to communicate with your intuitive wisdom. Visit *GoIntuition.com* for Free Downloads.

Free Go Intuition eNewsletter and Articles

Continue to be informed through signing up for your free Go Intuition eNewsletter. Each one embodies a nugget of truth that you can relate to immediately. You'll also find a host of thought provoking articles at *GoIntuition.com*.

Discover *Eureka!*

Eureka! Understanding and Using the Power of Your Intuition, by Anne Salisbury, PhD, is a valuable support. This analytical look at intuition includes thought provoking exercises you can apply immediately. In it you discover:

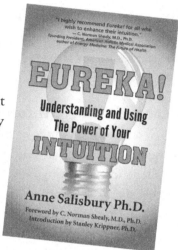

- What intuition is and is not
- How to tap into it
- How to trust it

You come to understand the meaning behind the all-encompassing definition of intuition. You delve into its history, the way it works in your life, what inhibits it and how techniques, such as meditation, self-hypnosis and dream work, encourage it. Everything you need to know about using your intuition is summed up in the easy-to-follow system of *ACT* and *LEAP*™. When applied, this can dramatically change your life:

Step 1: **A**sk for what you want
Step 2: **C**larify your desire
Step 3: Use **T**ools
Step 4: **L**et go
Step 5: **E**ureka!
Step 6: **A**ct on Eureka!
Step 7: **P**rove it

Visit *GoIntuition.com* or your local bookseller to order your copy today.

212

Discover *The Path of Intuition*

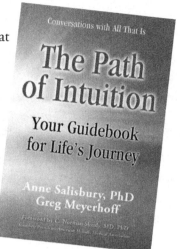

From an early age, Anne Salisbury saw and heard things that no one around her did. In church one morning, when she did not understand what the minister was saying, All That Is spoke up. "Jesus didn't say that . . ."

In *The Path of Intuition: Your Guidebook for Life's Journey,* Anne Salisbury, PhD, and Greg Meyerhoff have brought you the words of All That Is through Anne's extensive channelings. They help you find solutions to challenging situations so you can make decisions with confidence and ease.

- Access your intuition and higher wisdom.
- Discover answers to life's questions.
- Get unstuck and move ahead on your path.

This is a valuable companion book to *Journey to Heaven.* Through the words of All That Is, you gain a deep understanding of the true purpose of intuition.

Visit *GoIntuition.com* or your local bookseller to order your copy today.

Coming Soon...

Soon you will be able to learn more about life on the other side through Anne Salisbury and Greg Meyerhoff's next book, *Beyond Heaven: An Insider's Guide to the Afterlife*. They take you further into the afterlife to discover more about the intricacies you encounter there.

Next is *Stories from Pet Psychics: What Animals and Animal Communicators Want You to Know*. In this fascinating book, they share stories from their pet psychic readings and reveal the remarkable results they have witnessed through the many years of their practice. They also share how you can become an animal communicator yourself.

Lastly they bring you *Love Is All There Is: The Intuition Factor in Relationships*. In this book you will journey into your own heart where you can learn how to see relationships from an intuitive perspective. You will discover innovative ways to increase your intuitive abilities and develop fulfilling, enjoyable, and successful relationships.

For more upcoming books, visit *GoIntuition.com* and sign-up to receive your free eNewsletter.

CPSIA information can be obtained
at www.ICGtesting.com
Printed in the USA
LVOW04s2150170516

488753LV00030B/631/P